The
Unseen
Elderly

The Unseen Elderly

A Study of Marginally Subsistent Hotel Dwellers

J. Kevin Eckert

THE CAMPANILE PRESS
San Diego State University

J. Kevin Eckert
The Unseen Elderly
San Diego, California
The Campanile Press, San Diego State University
p xii 244

Hardback ISBN 0-916304-47-7
Paperback ISBN 0-916304-45-0

Designed by Rachael Bernier

THE CAMPANILE PRESS
San Diego State University
San Diego, California 92182

Dedicated to
Dorothy I. Eckert

Contents

LIST OF TABLES

LIST OF MAPS AND ILLUSTRATIONS

LIST OF FIGURES

Acknowledgements

Many people and organizations contributed to this book. The initial fieldwork was supported by a National Research Service Award from the National Institute of Mental Health. Additional support was provided through a research grant to the Western Behavioral Sciences Institute from the Center for Studies for Metropolitan Problems (NIMH). I thank these organizations for their support. Confidence, moral support, intellectual stimulation and cooperation came from many sides. Special thanks, however, must go to my friend, teacher and colleague, Paul Bohannan. Above all, I am grateful to the persons who became the focus of this study. Their lives have enriched my own.

Cleveland, Ohio
September 29, 1980

1

Introduction

The growing proportion of old people in technologically advanced societies has led to the recognition of aging as a social and scientific problem. The number of aged in today's society represents a cultural anomaly. For the first time in recorded history there exist in large numbers men and women already aged by established chronological standards who can anticipate another full decade or more of life.[1] Industrial societies have created a new group, yet the culture that brought the group into existence has not been able to incorporate them effectively into the social system.

In many respects, our institutions have failed to meet the needs of the older person. Concomitant with the awareness of the institutional failure, a literature on the plight of the older American has evolved. Much of this literature emphasizes the decrements of old age: loss of social relationships, roles, status, health, income. The continual concentration on "the problems of the elderly" and "the decrements of old age" tends to mask the successful adaptations of older persons to their environments and the great individual differences found among them.

While considerable research has been conducted on various sociological and psychological aspects of aging, few studies have provided us with detailed ethnographic descriptions of older persons in natural settings. A primary emphasis of this study is to provide an ethnographic description of an important living environment for older persons—single room occupancy (SRO) hotels in urban areas. It will focus on persons aged fifty years and over and the adaptations they make and supports they receive from the econiche in which they live. Such studies are necessary in order to gain an understanding of the processes of adaptation in old age.

Adaptive transactions are acted out at the microsocial level in the actual environments and social milieux in which older people live and function. There has been little study of the many different social environments in which particular kinds of elderly people live. Most studies of living environments have concentrated on institutional (nursing homes) or planned (retirement villages, public housing) settings. As Carp noted, "there is a scarcity of data on how most elderly people live, and much must be left to conjecture."[2] Thus, there is an urgent need to examine and describe the transactions between older people and their physical and social living environments (which include life-sustaining resources such as shops, eating places, medical care, and police protection as well as life enriching resources such as friends, family, and cultural opportunities).

Self-reliance and fear of dependence—its persistent psychological expression—are the *sine-qua-non* of the older SRO hotel population.[3] Their desire to remain independent and to provide for their own needs despite physical and economic hardship directs our attention toward modes of adjustment and coping styles. A concern for adaptive behavior further directs our attention to the articulation of human needs, purposes and wants with the environmental opportunities (and constraints) for satisfying those wants.

This present study is concerned with one particular type of housing—the urban hotels located in a deteriorating commercial zone in downtown San Diego, California. An ethnographic description of the hotel setting will help to explain the lifestyle of the older residents, their needs and problems, the opportunities and details of social support systems, social exchanges and concomitant modes of adjustment.

As we shall discover, different types of residents make distinctive patterns of adjustment to the setting, some more successfully than others. Success in the hotel setting frequently depends on the ability and skills of the older individual to optimize informal aspects of the setting so as to negotiate rewarding social exchanges. Thus, informal aspects of the hotel setting are described in relationship to their importance to the older hotel residents. As we have seen, a particularly important issue for the older resident is how to maintain the primary cultural values of self-reliance and independence in the face of mounting illness and disability. Therefore, a concern for the health status of the population emerges as a central problem.

Following the introduction, Chapter 2 will consider the position of the elderly in American society with particular focus on the elderly in urban context. The San Diego urban environment, its sociodemographic perspective, the various types of urban hotels, and the methodological approach to the study, are presented in Chapter 3. Primarily ethnographic in character, the study employed multiple methods, including participant observation, individual life histories, key informant interviews, and survey questionnaires. A general ethnographic description of one SRO hotel, the Ballentine,° is given in Chapter 4. Chapters 5 and 6 concern the caretakers and exploiters influencing the lives of the older hotel residents. Key persons inside the hotel, such as hotel staff, and those outside the hotel such as social/health agencies and community services are discussed. The social dimensions of the SRO world are delineated in Chapter 7. The various social groups and divisions within the hotel setting are examined. The interrelationship of economic restraints, dominant values, community supports, and modes of adjustment are discussed in Chapter 8. Chapter 9 focuses on the distinguishable life trajectory patterns of SRO residents. Chapter 10 involves health as an ever-present threat and underlying problem. Summary and conclusions follow in Chapter 11.

° This name, and other names of hotels and persons discussed in this book, are fictitious.

Conceptual Paradigms

In considering the adaptational processes of older persons in general, and in hotel residents in particular, two conceptual paradigms will prove useful: social exchange theory and human-environment optimization. Viewing social behavior as exchange has been set forth by such scholars as Homans, Blau and Emerson.[4] The basic assumption underlying exchange theory is that interactions between individuals and collectivities can be characterized as an attempt to maximize rewards (both material and non-material) and reduce costs (both material and non-material).[5] Dowd was among the first in gerontology to point out the importance of exchange theory for understanding the aging phenomenon in sociocultural terms. He suggests that,

> ... decreased social interaction in old age is a result, not only of previously mentioned conditions of widowhood, poor health, and lowered income, but also an intricate process of exchange between society and the aged resulting from their power dependent relationship.[6]

The aged are at a power disadvantage vis-a-vis society and are coerced or threatened to act in certain ways in order to avoid sanctions. For example, mandatory disengagement from work roles, with its concomitant decrease in income, exemplifies a process whereby the relative economic power[7] of the aged in relation to their environment is diminished. As Dowd so succinctly states, "where once the now retired worker was able to exchange expertise for needed wages, the final exchange required of most older workers would be their compliance (in the form of acquiescence to mandatory retirement) as exchange for sustenance (Social Security, Medicare, etc.)."[8]

Human behavior can be viewed as an exchange of more or less rewarding behaviors between two or more social actors. Exchange can also be viewed as transpiring between individuals and the larger sociophysical environment. From this perspective, the environment is seen to include not only psychological and social factors but those of the physical environment as well. That such features of the physical environment have a significant effect on individuals has been poignantly stated by James Birrens:

> Young adults, because they are agile, can adapt more easily to the increasingly scattered nature of urban functions. The mere reduced agility of the aged individual markedly reduces the life space available to him in the cities. It is easier for him if he moves into an older neighborhood with clustered small shops and narrow streets. Paradoxically, it is in the most deteriorated areas of cities that aged persons may live independent lives, piecing together for themselves the combination of needed services.[9]

Following Birren's observations, the study of the urban elderly necessitates that we define environment in the broadest terms.

The concept of environmental optimization pertains broadly to human transactions with the sociophysical environment, and is based on a feedback model of human behavior and cognition. The notion assumes that people ideally strive to achieve optimal environments, or those that maximize the fulfillment of their needs and the accomplishment of their goals and plans.[10] In reality, people are often forced by situational constraints to accept conditions which are not optimal in all respects. In such situations they must "satisfice"[11] —or achieve less than optimal improvements in their surroundings. As Stokols suggests, although environmental optimization is never realized in its ideal form, the concept is of heuristic value in emphasizing the goal-directed and cyclical nature of human-environment transactions.[12] Acceptance of this suggests that people seek situations or sociophysical environments where they can maximize their power advantage and minimize their costs.[13] The notion of environmental optimization is of crucial importance to studies of successful aging since it sensitizes us to the adaptive behaviors of older persons as they strive to meet their needs.

There is no question that this study's population—the elderly on fixed incomes living in urban hotels—has an overrepresentation of physical and emotional handicaps, low income, and limited opportunities. However, in the urban environment, they choose (within limits) a situation in which they can "make it." In the process of making it, older retirees can negotiate meaningful social exchanges to obtain needed goods and services. Not only is there a "fit" between the personal and psychological needs of individuals with their environment, but social structural variables such as values and norms of behavior are complementary to environmental demands. Within the single room occupancy hotel, many older persons are able to remain functional in spite of physical insults. Most importantly, they are able to remain independent and self-reliant—values of utmost importance to these older cohorts.[14]

Historical and Cultural Roots of Ageism

From a cultural and historical perspective the elderly have not always occupied a power-dependent position in society. Anthropological studies have helped to clarify the changing position of the aged, over time and across cultures.

The first comparative study of aging in various cultures was Leo Simmons's *The Role of the Aged in Primitive Societies.*[15] Drawing data from the Yale Human Relations Area File on seventy-one "primitive peoples" Simmons demonstrated the unsurprising conclusion that the status of the aged varied among societies. He found that the allocation of resources and honor to older persons in a given society was negatively related to the development of technology and occupational specialization. The aged of pre-industrial/agricultural society were able to accumulate and control a much larger share of power resources than their post-industrial/urban society counterparts. A major collection of papers edited by Cowgill and Holmes, *Aging and Modernization,* further corroborated Simmons's conclusions.[16]

In their book, Cowgill and Holmes develop a rudimentary theory of aging in a cross cultural perspective. Their collection of papers supports several generalizations concerning the status of the aged in differing societies. At the most general level they found that the concept of old age appears to be relative to the degree of modernizations. In more "primitive" societies where life spans are relatively limited the onset of old age occurs earlier. In many societies a person is defined as old by the age of forty-five to fifty years. By contrast, in more modern societies old age is thought to begin at or about age sixty. Cowgill and Holmes proposed several propositions concerning the status of the aged. First and most importantly, they found the status of the aged inversely proportional to the rate of social change. This proposition is best summarized by Simmons:

> In the long and steady studies of the social order, the aging get themselves fixed and favored in positions, power and performance. They have what we call seniority rights. But when social conditions become unstable and the rate of change reaches a galloping pace, the aged are riding for an early fall and the more youthful associates take their seats in the saddle.[17]

A second set of propositions closely related to the first states that the status of the aged is bolstered among agricultural peoples as a result of stability of residence coupled with the highly developed concepts of land ownership. The ability of people to maintain their property rights into old age provides not only economic security but also prestige and power. Also, such "folk" societies tend to emphasize tradition and ceremonialism. In such societies, those persons who are best versed in the traditions and who know the proper ceremonial forms are likely to be the older people.[18] If the society is preliterate, the status of the aged is further enhanced by their role as the repositories of knowledge and tradition; they are pivotal in information storage and transmission.

An additional set of propositions maintains that the status of the aged was higher in those societies where the extended form of family was prevalent and lower in societies which favored the nuclear form of family. In general this means a stronger familial role for the elderly in non-industrial societies and a weaker position and less family involvement for older people in modern societies. Thus, with the onset of the industrial revolution and concomitant advances in technology and specialization of knowledge, the aged found themselves having less to offer. Expressing this same notion, Dowd concludes,

> The actual crafts or trade or the more general expertise of leadership and experience which sufficed as barter in exchanges of long ago are no longer considered rewarding. Consequently, whatever power advantage they once occupied gradually shifted to others in the society. And, as the growth rate increased in exponential leaps and bounds, the relative power of the aged decreased further as the resultant surfeit of available labor decreased their range of available employment opportunities.[19]

With the extension of the life span and the exclusion of older persons from what society has labeled "productive" roles, the problem of powerlessness became further complicated by a lack of defined social norms and roles for the elderly. Whereas the norms and tasks associated with youth and adulthood have been delineated and specified, those of old age have not. Thus, in present-day American society, many of the responsibilities that mark adulthood are relinquished (through legitimated societal norms) at a time when the individual can still expect to live several more decades. The extension of the life span beyond the "productive" years creates a life period devoid of social meaning, and increased economic and social dependence. Therefore, the roots of many problems of older persons in our culture lie in the normlessness of this newly extended life epoch.[20]

Clark and Anderson give four principal historical factors that have influenced the normlessness of the elderly in Western contemporary society: the weakness of kinship ties; the rapidity of industrial and technological change; the phenomenal increase in the number of older persons in American society; and finally, heavy American emphasis on the value of productivity and work.[21]

Contrary to popular belief, evidence is mounting that the extended and multigenerational family was never the prevailing mode in America.[22] It is likely that the aged in the

United States have "always" been more spatially separated from their children, grandchildren, and other relatives than have older persons in Europe and most other parts of the world. Coupled with the relative exclusion of the American aged from the supposed benefits of the extended family is the growing tendency for segregation of the elderly into separate communities.

As mentioned earlier, rapid industrial and technological change have institutionalized obsolescence as a part of growing old. Progress in technology and automation quickly date the knowledge and skill many older adults mastered early in their careers. The older worker finds it increasingly difficult to avoid layoffs and, once unemployed, to find a job.[23] As a result, an increasing portion of older persons believe themselves to be of little value in modern Western life.

Related to the rapid increase in technological change is the dominant emphasis in American culture on productivity and work. As Kluckhohn once stated,

> Americans are not merely optimistic believers that work counts. Their creed insists that everyone, anywhere in the social structure, can and should "make the effort"...The only way to be safe in American life is to be a success. Failure to "measure up" is felt as deep personal inadequacy.[24]

The ability of the older adult to "measure up" is affected by the premium placed on training and education. The increased need for training and education has greatly prolonged the time Americans spend preparing for adulthood. Thus, older people in contemporary America are generally more poorly trained and educated than younger people. Older persons also face a plethora of negative stereotypes and expectations about older workers as a category. While it is true that some older persons become impaired physically or mentally and are forced to leave the work force, many retired workers are not impaired.[25] Bureaucratic rules and cultural definitions of "old age" arbitrarily exclude most older individuals from the work force. When social sanctions levied against older workers impinge on the individual's self-image, a struggle for adjustment follows.

Compounding the problems of unemployment and lack of productive activity is the increasing number of persons in the society aged sixty-five years old and over. The aging of the American population is not a new phenomenon, but one that has been progressing for as long as vital statistics have been collected. According to Hauser, one in ten persons is presently sixty-five years old and over and the prospect is that it will be one in six in the not-too-distant future. He notes that the number and value of older people was enhanced in the "little" community by the fact of their scarcity. This value is lost in "mass" society. Thus, the prestige of older persons is diminished even further.[26]

The changing demographic structure of Western industrial society rang the alarm for those who realize the implications and strains a larger older population would create for the health and welfare systems. Pollak in a Social Science Research Council report noted that contemporary demographic trends were "fraught with social implications" especially in societies which historically value competition, extol individuality, stress productivity, are deeply suspicious of public welfare programs, experience changes in the structure and function of families, and insist on universalistic standards of performance regardless of age. On the basis of these factors, the aged in America face a dilemma. They are rendered helpless, either by personal default or social definition, to meet cultural ideals—consequently, they are devalued.[27]

These historical factors have helped to create a situation in Western and urbanized industrial nations that devalues the older person and his place in the social structure. These factors contribute to what Robert Butler has termed ageism—the social practices (including prejudices and stereotypes) which are negative in their appraisal of older persons and their roles in society.[28]   With the historical roots of ageism in mind, let us now turn attention to the present conditions of the older person in American society.

Notes

1   M. Clark, "Pattern of Aging Among the Elderly Poor of the Inner City," *The Gerontologist* (Spring, 1971, Part II):78.

2   F.M. Carp, "Housing and Living Environments of Older People," in *Handbook of Aging and the Social Sciences,* ed. R.H. Binstock and E. Shanas (New York: Van Nostrand Reinhold Company, 1976), p. 252.

3   F.L.K. Hsu, "American Core Value and National Character," in *Psychological Anthropology,* new edition (Cambridge, Mass.: Schenkman Publishing Co., 1959), p. 249. The importance of self-reliance, independence and autonomy as core American values is supported by considerable research. In addition to this article by Hsu, see also his *Psychological Anthropology: Approaches to Culture and Personality* (Homewood, Illinois: Dorsey Press, 1961); M. Mead, *And Keep Your Powder Dry* (New York: William Morrow and Company, 1943); and G. Gorer, *The American People: A Study in National Character* (New York: W.W. Norton Company, 1945).

4   G. Homans, *The Human Group* (New York: Harcourt Brace, 1950); P.M. Blau, Exchange and Power in Social Life (New York: J. Wiley, 1964); R.M. Emmerson, "Power-dependence relations," *American Sociological Review* 27 (1962):31-41.

5   E.E. Knipe, "Attraction and exchange: Some temporal considerations," paper presented at the annual meeting of the Sociological Society, Atlanta, 1971.

6   J.J. Dowd, "Aging and exchange: A preface to theory," *Journal of Gerontology,* 30, no. 5 (1975):584-594.

7   Social exchange theorists view power as a derivative of imbalanced exchange. It is based on the inability of one actor in a social exchange to reciprocate a rewarding behavior.

8   Dowd, "Aging," p. 587.

9   J.E. Birren, "The Abuse of the Urban Aged," *Psychology Today,* 3, no. 10 (1970):37.

10   D. Stokols, "Environmental Psychology," *Annual Review of Psychology* 29(1978):253-95.

11   H.A. Simon, *Models of Man: Explorations in the Western Educationl Tradition* (New York: Wiley, 1957).

12   D. Stokols, "Environmental Psychology."

13   Exchange theorists would argue that the partner in a social exchange who is less dependent on that exchange for the gratification he seeks enjoys a power advantage. See Dowd, "Aging," p. 588. In its simplest form, the term "costs" refers to the negative value or unpleasantness actually experienced in the course of obtaining a reward.

14   M. Clark and B.G. Anderson, Culture and Aging (Springfield: Charles C. Thomas, 1967); P.J. Bohannan and J.K. Eckert, *Food and Food-Related Health of Old People in Center City Hotels* (La Jolla: Western Behavioral Sciences Institute, 1976); P. Ehrlich, *St. Louis's "Invisible Elderly": Needs and Characteristics of Aged Single-Room Occupancy Downtown Hotel Residents* (St. Louis Institute of Applied Gerontology, St. Louis University, 1976); B.J. Stephens, *Loners, Losers and Lovers: Elderly Tenants in a Slum Hotel* (Seattle: University of Washington Press, 1976); R.J. Erickson and J.K. Eckert, "The Elderly Poor in Downtown San Diego Hotels, *Gerontologist* 17:5 (1977):440-446.

15   L.W. Simmons, *The Role of the Aged in Primitive Societies* (New Haven: Yale University Press, 1945).

16   D.O. Cowgill and L.D. Holmes, eds., *Aging and Modernization* (New York: Appleton-Century-Crofts, 1972).

17   Simmons, *Role*, p. 177.

18   R. Redfield, *The Little Community* (Chicago: University of Chicago Press, 1953).

19   Dowd, "Aging," p. 588.

20   M. Clark and B.G. Anderson, *Culture and Aging* (Springfield: Charles C. Thomas, 1967), p. 10.

21   Ibid.

22   E.A. Friedmann, "The Impact of Aging on the Social Structure," in *The Handbook of Social Gerontology*, ed. C. Tibbitts (Chicago: University of Chicago Press, 1960); J.C. Beresford and A.M. Rivlin, "The Multigenerational Family," mimeographed paper prepared for a meeting on Multigenerational Family at the University of Michigan Conference on Aging, Ann Arbor, 1969.

23   H.L. Sheppard, "Work and Retirement," in *Handbook of Aging and the Social Sciences*, ed. R.H. Binstock and E. Shanas (New York: Van Nostrand Reinhold Company, 1976), p. 298.

24   C. Kluckhohn, *Mirror for Man* (New York: Whittlesey House, 1949), pp. 233-236.

25   Research findings on the job performance of older persons are presently difficult to interpret because of differences in method, population studied, and theoretical approaches. However, recent studies of actual job performance evaluations reveal findings favorable to the older worker. Some studies indicate that in many areas (e.g., consistency of output) the older worker out-performs the younger worker. For additional information see Sheppard, "Work and Retirement," pp. 286-309.

26   P.M. Hauser, "Aging and World-wide Population Change," in *Handbook of Aging and the Social Sciences*, ed. R.H. Binstock and E. Shanas (New York: Van Nostrand Reinhold Company), p. 81.

27   Clark and Anderson, *Culture and Aging*, pp. 13-18.

28   R.N. Butler, "Ageism: Another Form of Bigotry," *Gerontologist*, 9 (1969).

2

The Urban Social Environment
and the Aged

In 1970, the majority of older persons (14.6 million, or 73 percent) lived in urban areas. Of these urban elderly, more than half (55 percent) were located in heavily urbanized areas, with 6.8 million of these in central cities.[1] Older people are disproportionately concentrated in the central cities. This fact makes urban issues such as congestion, transportation, living costs, crime, and housing of major concern for those interested in the health and well-being of older persons.

Louis Wirth defined the city as "... a relatively large, dense and permanent settlement of socially heterogeneous individuals."[2] Moreover, according to Wirth, cities are a way of life where human relationships are anonymous, transitory, and superficial:

> Characteristically, urbanities meet one another in highly segmental roles. They ... are dependent upon more people for the satisfaction of their life needs than are rural people ... but they are less dependent on particular persons ....

He then added:

> The reserve, the indifference and the blase outlook which

urbanities manifest in their relationships may be regarded as devices for immunizing themselves against the personal claims and expectations of others.[3]

Wirth's statement and especially his unproved, indeed, unexamined, addendum on the anomic character of cities has followed the manner in which society and such scholars as Durkheim and Tonnies have chosen to deal with urban centers.[4] Jacobs remarked that, "unstudied, unrespected, cities have served as sacrificial victims."[5] Not only have the physical aspects of cities been viewed critically (e.g., Riesman's images of inner-city traffic, congestion, noise, pollution, and deteriorating structures),[6] but the single urban lifestyle has been characterized frequently as shallow and fragmented.[7]

Clark points out that cities are housing not only more and more ethnic populations, but increasing numbers of aging people as well. These trends are clearly the result of deterioration in the quality of life in the urban core areas. The aged have not been able to join in the flight of the younger affluents to suburbia to avoid the noise, smog, dirt, and other social tensions associated with city life.[8] Both minority and aged groups are locked into the urban environment by a complexity of factors, not the least of which is inexpensive housing provided by tenements, cheap hotels, and furnished rooms.

The plight of the urban aged has been expounded by several scholars. Brice suggests that, too poor to join the rush to the suburbs, the urban aged remain trapped in the central city where they are exploited by landlords, robbed by thugs, and ignored by almost everyone else.[9] They remain lonely, and isolated in hotels, apartments, and boarding houses.[10] In this regard, Margaret Clark has made the most vivid assertion:

> . . . the inner city elderly are, both physically and psychologically sicker than their age peers in other groups. They have a harder time surviving—perhaps the hardest of any elderly cohort we know. No one lovingly watches over the destinies of these tough survivors. They survive by their wits, like the rats that are often their only company.[11]

In contrast to the view emphasizing the "plight" of the urban aged is the view that, granting the existence of hardships and deprivation, the center city provides compensations not available to the aged poor in other locales. Niebanck and Pope reflect:

> It is a curious thing that the high density urban areas that are being abandoned by many younger households, contain elements that make life easier and more pleasurable for the elderly. The young are automobile users and space consumers. The elderly are quite the opposite. Many of the characteristics that would be considered incompatible with a suburban development are for the elderly the very things that contribute to efficiency and comfort.[12]

As noted earlier, the most deteriorated sections of the city often provide the only places in which the aged and the poor can piece together the goods and services necessary to continue independent living.[13]

Until recently, the aged poor in the inner city have been little studied as a discrete group. Gerontological research has centered on aged persons easily reached through institutional affiliations such as senior centers, retirement villages, "golden age clubs," hospitals, or old age homes. Also lacking are small scale microstudies of select econiches or "socioniches."[14] Clark attributes this lack of interest to the unglamorous nature of elderly city poor, who are usually of European ethnicity. However, numerous studies have pointed to the inner city elderly as a unique population among the aging.[15]

Single Room Occupancy Hotels and the Urban Aged

James Spradley in his study of "urban nomads" emphasized the plight of American cities as well as their viability as a "melting pot." In our urban centers the pluralistic character of American society is most evident. As Spradley suggests:

> Americans do not simply belong to different generations, classes, racial or ethnic groups, they have also acquired distinct values, goals, and life-styles—they come from different subcultures.[16]

The past few years have seen a small, but steadily growing interest in the subculture of persons living alone in downtown hotels and rooming houses. A population of older persons who have traditionally lived alone and characterized themselves as "loners" is to be found in most American cities. For them, hotels in downtown commercial areas have provided the shelter and services to meet personal needs. Phyllis Ehrlich has aptly characterized this nonfamily elderly component as distinct from other elderly persons.[17]

Presently many downtown urban areas are undergoing change—many deteriorating buildings are the target of urban renewal. Because the older hotels are located in these marginal slum or tenderloin areas, renewal projects are decreasing their number. As a consequence, the downtown elderly, among the most limited both in income and in coping resources, find themselves with fewer housing options and supportive neighborhoods. The lack of interest in this group of elderly is disturbing in light of evidence that an increasing number of the aged are choosing to live in converted hotels.[18]

Awareness of persons living in single room occupancy hotels, rooming houses, and apartments has been intermittently apparent since the 1920s. Zorbaugh focused on the unique social situation afforded by the rooming house. He characterized the "dwellers in furnished rooms" as a socially isolated and anomic type:

> The roomers do not know one another. People come and go without speaking or questioning. Anonymity is well-nigh complete. In this situation of mobility and anonymity the person is socially isolated. His wishes are thwarted. He finds in the rooming house neither security, response nor recognition. He is restless and he is lonely.[19]

Hayner added to the recognition of hotel life as atomistic in nature. He attributed the lack of social solidarity among tenants of urban hotels to an emphasis on individual goals and interests at the expense of developing communal goals. He also stressed the social isolation, impersonality, and anonymity of the hotel life-style. This view gained further support by Rose.[20]

Lawton and Kleban and Clark in a two-part series for *The Gerontologist* gave a useful overview of aged residents of the inner-city and their patterns of aging. Lawton and Kleban concentrated on the life-styles of poor Jewish tenants residing in a section of Philadelphia known as "Strawberry Mansion." The once prestigious Strawberry Mansion area is now a low-income high-crime area. They discovered that by almost all indices of well-being, the older residents were markedly deprived compared to members of their age cohorts in other contexts. The residents of Strawberry Mansion were more likely to be single or widowed, with grossly lower incomes. Additionally, compared to other samples of older persons, "... they are deprived in the areas of health, neighborhood motility, leisure-time activity, peer interaction, morale, and housing satis-faction."[21] In spite of their physical, economic, and social handicaps, older residents of Strawberry Mansion are coping. However, "ordinary coping behavior requires energy expenditure at a near-upper threshold level."[22] Accordingly, the life-chances of these elderly are severely limited. They are locked into their environment due to low income and comparatively low rents; their life space is restricted and they have few contacts with neighbors and relatives. The results of the Lawton and Kleban study showed that environmental factors had a substantial and unique association with neighborhood motility and interviewers' ratings of vigor, interaction, and responsiveness. As much previous research has shown, health is by far the most potent predictor of well-being.[23]

Margaret Clark's "Patterns of Aging Among the Elderly Poor of the Inner City" gives rich insight and observations about urban environments and their potential for promoting both human misery and human survival. She cites one of the central themes of the present study—the examination of informal structure and support systems:

> One of the more promising approaches to social planning for the inner-city aged ... is to examine the ways in which the aged poor, when faced with the basic problems of physical and psychological survival, develop informal structures for their solution.[24]

Joan Shapiro has devoted considerable attention to the specific characteristics of single room occupancy tenants in New York City, where an estimated 100,000 persons live in such tenements.[25] The term single room occupancy (SRO) originated in New York and refers to tenement apartment buildings that have been converted to living quarters for unattached poor people. In effect, they are slum hotels providing transient and permanent homes for alcoholics, addicts, prostitutes, petty criminals, the indigent chronically ill, mentally retarded adults, and the elderly—all who cannot care adequately for themselves in the larger society. An overwhelming number of the tenants receive welfare and over 50 percent are alcoholic.[26] Violence is endemic and contributes to a mutual distrust and fear among residents. Shapiro identified three groups (winos, addicts, and "mentals") who related on the basis of common pathology. A common pattern found in the SROs Shapiro studied was the formation of groups around dominant females.

> The most common constellation is the matriarchal quasi-family, in which the dominant women tend to feed, protect, punish, and set norms for the alcoholic "family" members. They share some meals, and the room of the leader is a hub of continuous social activity .... The members of the group have kinship names ... tend to be middle aged, physically sick, and more psychologically dependent. Sometimes, nonalcoholic, mentally ill people or retarded individuals attach themselves to these families and are cared for in them. The matriarch, herself usually an alcoholic, has much power to dictate both the behavior of the family members and their relationship to each other.[27]

Shapiro discovered that managers and tenants of the SRO become locked into a common reciprocal relationship characterized by mutual dependence. This dependence extends beyond the economics of the situation to emotional and ritual ties, enactments, and altercations. Landlords and managers are assured a steady flow of welfare dollars from a welfare population that cannot leave. In return, the tenants are granted a permissiveness which allows the acting-out of socially deviant behavior which would not be tolerated in other settings.

Relationships among tenants are characterized by a wide spectrum of acted out feelings, punctuated by short-lived crises. Friendship, while often intense, is fleeting over time.[28]

The culture of the SRO was found to be:

> ...sensory, immediate, spontaneous, auditory, and action oriented as opposed to logical, reflective, visual. Communications favor the nonverbal over the verbal.... Tenants habitually use touch to communicate feeling.... Gesture, posture, and facial expression, too, convey vivid messages.[29]

Finally, she summarized the tenants of the SROs as sullen and passive, the latter brought on by disease, malnutrition, and limited life-chances.

Harvey Siegal has recently completed another study of SRO tenements in New York City.[30] His study focuses on the collective patterns and adaptation capable of sustaining life in an actively hostile environment. He argues that the SRO is a discrete entity with a specific "community." This notion counters earlier work done on hotel life which emphasized that the SRO was not a social world.[31] Siegal says that these earlier researchers started from the wrong premise—that the notion of social disorganization blinded them to the richness of social life in the SRO.

Siegal's study population consisted of older, predominantly nonwhite individuals "...so frequently demonstrating severe health and social problems as to make regular, gainful employment problematic."[32] He chose the perspectives of: (1) the culture of poverty, (2) community, and (3) social deviance as the most appropriate conceptual framework for dealing with the population and the environment. He divided the SRO population into two groups: first, older permanent residents, usually white, who had lived in the building for more than a decade; and second, and more numerous than the first group, those new to the city, minority groups, the alienated and the chronically ill.[33] Siegal gave very little attention to the first group—the predominately white older residents, who are our primary research population.

Therefore, Siegal's theorizing was meant to apply primarily to the second population. Unfortunately, his book and others can be (and usually are) read in such a way that his analysis of the deviants is applied to all, including the nondeviant elderly. The ideas about "focus on adjustment" may be convenient for both the subpopulations, but the idea of deviance certainly applies only to the first.

In concluding, Siegal postulates that the SRO will become increasingly important as the more traditional ways of handling our "socially terminal" people gradually vanish or are radically changed.

> As a viable, specialized, fully integrated, naturally occurring social phenomenon, it (the SRO) relieves the state of the responsibility of caring for these kinds of social casualties .... They provide indigenous care for those who are either incapable of caring for themselves, or those who find social participation in an open setting problematic.[34]

Overall, the work of Joyce Stephens supports other research on the SRO elderly.[35] Stephens's work was carried out in a single hotel located in the deteriorating inner core of Detroit. The individuals with whom she worked had personal histories reflecting alienation, deviance, and low degrees of involvement in the conventional institutions of American society.[36] Residents included petty thieves, alcoholics, addicts, hustlers, unattached urban poor, and the down and outers. A large proportion of these persons were not new to the SRO environment, but had spent their entire adult lives working and living in the area,

> They experienced no sudden, catastrophic event that catapulted them into the atomistic alienated world of the SRO. Rather, they have gradually, but inexorably been settling in for a long time.[37]

She found that the residents, especially the aged ones, had "tarnished identities" when viewed from the perspective of the larger society.

Certain identifying characteristics of Stephens's SRO

population include: a higher proportion of single individual's, extreme poverty and a concentration of physical and mental handicaps. Life spaces were severely limited, often not extending beyond the confines of the room or hotel. Tenants were locked into the hotel by the twin determinants of low rent and low income. Dominant features of the SRO included severe forms of isolation, depersonalization, and the institutionalization of mutual suspicion.[38]

Personal relationships were found to be "problematic." As "loners," SRO people had broken all ties with family and friends: "They live in a world marked by the extremes of alienation, isolation, and anonymity."[39] Stephens attributes the utilitarian and noninvolved nature of interpersonal relationships to the SRO resident's personal need for security in a noxious and threatening environment. Avoidance of close ties is an institutionalized norm enabling these elderly people to anticipate and mobilize to meet potentially destructive events and situations.[40]

Stephens makes the strongest case for the alienated and anomic life-style of the elderly SRO resident. While there is little doubt that the particularily noxious environment in which the older residents live contributed to their fear of forming close interpersonal relationships, she fails to consider the issue of isolation and lack of investment in others as a pattern of life-long adjustment. It is likely that the isolation found among some older hotel residents has been a lifelong pattern and not a specific response to the vicissitudes of hotel living. Additionally, her particular explanation overlooks the possibility of various personality types being subsumed under what appears to be a singular lifestyle characterized by living alone in low priced hotels.

Phyllis Ehrlich, formerly at the Institute for Applied Gerontology of St. Louis University, has looked into the lifestyles of the SROs in downtown St. Louis.[41] Ehrlich's study reaffirms many of the points made by Shapiro, Stephens, Siegal, and others. However, her findings concerning the health of residents contradict the stereotypical conceptions. Instead of being a sick and needy people, Ehrlich's study population expressed only a slight bother with sickness. She found people with a low perceived incidence of heart disease, arthritis, and hypertension. Stress related diseases such as nervousness, headaches, and high blood pressure were not significantly present.

Most importantly, Ehrlich's findings support the notion of a distinct downtown hotel personality. The study suggests that there is:

> A distinct SRO personality type and lifestyle built on a pattern of existence detached from other people and social systems. A choice of the downtown "single room only" residence and a preference for the lifestyle. A strong interrelationship between SRO personality and environmental factors which serves to strengthen the preference.[42]

The findings suggest that at least a segment of the downtown population forms a discrete category of people—though not an homogeneous group.

Ehrlich found an unmistakable relationship between lack of investment of self in sociality and low incidence of stress-related illnesses. This correlation suggests that the SRO resident's coping mechanism under the pressures of modern urban society is to deny physical symptoms and environmental stresses. While denial might be considered maladaptive for some populations, Ehrlich says it can be viewed as a positive adjustment for SRO residents.

In spite of the geronotological literature relating positive mental health to the number of confidantes in one's social circle, Ehrlich found that, "SROs appear psychologically adjusted in spite of minimal social interaction or lack of close friends."[43] She found a pattern of consistent noninvolvement, in which there was immense social distance between persons living in proximity.

Ehrlich judged the primary support system of SRO residents to be superficial and quite dependent on the role of the hotel desk clerk. Like Stephens, she attributed the utilitarian nature of social relationships to a fear of becoming vulnerable to exploitation.[44]

Maintenance of good health was found to be of utmost importance to SRO residents because it furthered the individualistic lifestyle within the hotel environment. However, while health was a priority, the residents were found to minimize and postpone the use of health care services. There was a generalized pattern of low usage and involvement in community systems and services.

Social ecology data suggest that even though the city offers a plethora of services and resources, the SRO resident uses only those that are vital for daily living. This minimal use of services points to a "routinized social life in an area that could allow for much interaction or anonymity."[45]

Ehrlich asserted clearly that the SRO lifestyle is chosen. She concluded that the downtown environment and the hotels that house the SRO population make possible and allow continuation of this lone pattern of living.

Health information on the SRO population is contra-dictory. On the one hand, the older residents of downtown hotels and rooming houses are characterized as being in exceedingly

Health information on the SRO population is contra-dictory. On the one hand, the older residents of downtown hotels and rooming houses are characterized as being in exceedingly poor physical and emotional health.[46] On the other hand, findings are emerging that indicate a population with low perceived health difficulties and needs.[47]

These contradictory findings probably relate to the differing definitions and methods utilized in assessing health status as well as the character of the groups studied. For example, Shapiro, Siegal and Stephens based their assessment of health on observational methods and did not incorporate objective or self-perceived indices of health in their studies. Both Shapiro and Siegal give little data on the health status of the older hotel dwellers per se. The tenement hotels they studied had large percentages of nonwhites with what they called "spoiled identities" and "deviant lifestyles." Thus, the cohort of older, nondeviants was not separated out and was not considered in detail.[48]

Stephens focused on the older hotel dweller and mentioned health as a major concern for them. But she gave little data on the scope or intricacies of the problem. Her focal statement on health reads:

> An underlying factor that influences the ability of these people to manage in their setting is the status of their health. Disabilities and handicaps abound. In addition, they are susceptible to falls and injuries. More pertinent to our understanding of their behavior is their attitude toward various physical and mental handicaps. The tenuous status of their health constitutes a major source of anxiety for them. They equate illness with old age; infirmity is the essence of old age. To maintain reasonable good health is to keep at bay old age with its implications of dependency.[49]

Ehrlich and Tissue utilized measures of self-perceived health status on randomly selected samples of older hotel residents and found relatively high levels of functional health. For example, Tissue in a comparison of suburban and downtown males found that the latter exhibited a remarkably high level of functional health and seemed immune to the kinds of problems and concerns that depress morale in the suburban group. More importantly, his data suggested a distinctive lifestyle for the downtown men, one in which what he called "morale" was unaffected by comparative social isolation, minimal fixed income, and a desire to have a job again. The older poor men who live in the central city differ from those living in surrounding areas in terms of living arrangement, marriage and family, contacts with other people, responses to poverty, mobility, and health, and recreational activity.[50]

> Downtown men led mobile, marginal lives in the past. They seldom married, produced few children, and are currently unlikely to see those whom they did father. They live alone in hotels, rooming houses and other rented quarters. They see tradespeople, neighbors and acquaintances, but have few close friends or relatives. They are, however, exceptionally healthy, find their income adequate to their needs, and take advantage of their proximity to urban facilities for recreation, amusement, and transportation.[51]

In contrast, suburban men were found to be family men, with homes and children.

These findings lead Tissue to the conclusion that the central city is not merely a set of conditions to which older persons are randomly assigned, but instead, "it represents the choice or destination of a special group of men whose biographies, activities, and needs set them at sharp variance from those who wind up living elsewhere."[52]

Notes

1   D. Woodruff and J. Birren, *Aging: Scientific Perspectives and Social Issues* (New York: Van Nostrand Co., 1975), pp. 55.

2   L. Wirth, "Urbanism as a Way of Life," *American Journal of Sociology,* 44, no. 1 (1938):8.

3   Ibid., 12.

4   E. Durkheim, *The Division of Labor in Society* (New York: Free Press, 1947, originally published, 1883); F. Tonnies, *Community and Society (Gemeinschaft und Gesellschaft)* trans. C.P. Loomis (New York: Harper and Row, 1963, originally published 1883).

5   J. Jacobs, *The Death and Life of Great American Cities* (New York: Vintage Books, 1961), p. 14.

6   D. Reisman, "The Suburban Dislocation," *The Annals,* 34(1957).

7   G. Simmel, *The Sociology of George Simmel,* ed. (New York: MacMillan, 1950) *Die Grossstadte und das Geisitesleben Die Geistesleben Die Grosstadte, 1900* Wirth, "Urbanism."

8   M. Clark, "Pattern of Aging Among the Elderly Poor of the Inner City," *The Gerontologist* (Spring, 1971, Part II):58; J.E. Birren, "The Abuse of the Urban Aged," *Psychology Today, 3, no. 10 (1970):37-38.*

9   D. Brice, "The Geriatric Ghetto," *San Francisco,* 12, no. 9 (1970).

10 C. Tibbitts and J.L. Schmelzer, "New Directions in Aging and Their Research Implications," *Welfare in Review,* 3, no. 2 (1965).

11   Clark, "Pattern of Aging," p. 59.

12   P.L. Niebanck and J. Pope, *The Elderly in Older Urban Areas: Problems of Adaptation and the Effects of Relocation* (Philadelphia: Institute for Environmental Studies, University of Pennsylvania, 1963), p. 137.

13   H.M. Bahr, "The Gradual Disappearance of Skid Row," *Social Problems*, 15, no. 1 (1867); Birren, "Abuse;" P.J. Bohannan and J.K. Eckert, *Food and Food-Related Health of Old People in Center City Hotels* (La Jolla, Ca.: Western Behavioral Sciences Institute, 1976).

14   Clark, "Pattern of Aging," p. 58.

15   See, for example, B. Bild and R. Havighurst, "Senior Citizens in Great Cities: The Case of Chicago," *The Gerontologist*, 16, no. 1, Part II (1976); M. Clark and B.G. Anderson, *Culture and Aging* (Springfield: Charles C. Thomas, 1967); M.F. Lowenthal, "Social Isolation and Mental Illness in Old Age," *American Sociological Review*, 29, no. 1 (1964); M.F. Lowenthal, P.L. Berkman and associates, *Aging and Mental Disorders in San Francisco* (San Francisco: Jossey-Bass, 1967); J.H. Shapiro, *Communities of the Alone* (New York: Association Press, 1971); H. Siegal, *Outposts of the Forgotten: Lifeways of Socially Terminal in Slum Hotels and Single Room Occupancy Tenements* (New Jersey: Transaction Books, 1978); B.J. Stephens, *Loners, Losers, and Lovers: Elderly Tenants in a Slum Hotel* (Seattle: University of Washington Press, 1976).

16   J. Spradley, *You Owe Yourself a Drunk* (Boston: Little, Brown, 1970), p. 4.

17   P. Ehrlich, *St. Louis "Invisible" Elderly Needs and Characteristics of Aged "Single Room Occupancy" Downtown Hotel Residents* (St. Louis: Institute of Applied Gerontology, St. Louis University, 1976), p. 7.

18   Stephens, *Loners, Losers and Lovers.*

19   H.W. Zorbaugh, *The Golden Coast and the Slums* (Chicago: University of Chicago Press, 1926, p. 101.

20   N.S. Hayner, *Hotel Life* (Asheville, North Carolina: University of North Carolina Press, 1936); A.M. Rose, "Interest in the Living Arrangement of the Urban Unattached," *American Journal of Sociology*, 53 (1948).

21   M.P. Lawton and M.H. Kleban, "The Aged Resident of the Inner City," *The Gerontologist*, 11 (Winter, 1971); Clark "Patterns of Aging."

22   Lawton and Kleban, "Aged Resident," p. 280.

23   M.P. Lawton, "Social Ecology and the Health of the Older People,"
        American Journal of Public Health, 64, no. 3 (1974); H.S. Maas and
        J.A. Kuypers, *From Thirty to Seventy* (San Francisco: Jossey-Bass,
        1974).

24   Clark, "Pattern of Aging," p. 64.

25   J.H. Shapiro, "Single Room Occupancy: Community of the Alone,"
        Social Work, 11 (October, 1966); "Dominant Leaders Among Slum
        Hotel Residents," *American Journal of Orthopsychiatry*, 39 (July,
        1969); "Reciprocal Dependence Between Single-Room Occupancy
        Managers and Tenants," *Social Work*, 15 (July, 1970); *Communities of
        the Alone* (New York: Association Press, 1971). The source for the
        statistic is R. Jorgens, "An Intimate Glimpse into the Life of the SRO
        Elderly." Paper presented at the Second Annual Conference on SRO
        Elderly, St. Louis University Institute of Applied Gerontology, May,
        1976.

26   Shapiro, *Communities*, p. 15.

27   Ibid., p. 25.

28   Ibid., p. 32. M.W. Riley and A. Foner, *Aging and Society*, vol. 1, *An
        Inventory of Research Findings* (New York: Russell Sage Foundation)
        and M.F. Lowenthal and B. Robinson, "Social Networks and Isolation,"
        in *Handbook of Aging and the Social Sciences*, ed. R.H. Binstock and
        E. Shanas (New York: Van Nostrand Reinhold Company, 1976) report
        that the findings on the friendship patterns of older persons in
        Western countries are scattered and ambiguous. However, Riley and
        Foner (p. 561) make several inferences: (1) Friendship and neighborly
        relations tend to be maintained well into later life; (2) the higher the
        status of the older persons, the more likely they are to have friends;
        (3) the longer the person has lived in the same neighborhood, the
        more extensive the ties to neighbors and friends become; (4) older
        people tend to have friends who are similar to themselves in status
        characteristics that affect common experience and values.

29   Shapiro, *Communities*, p. 29.

30   Siegal, *Outposts of the Forgotten*.

31   H.W. Zorbaugh, *Golden Coast;* N.S. Hayner, *Hotel Life*.

32   Siegal, *Outposts of the Forgotten*, p. 190.

33   Ibid., p. 180.

34   Ibid., p. 193.

35   Stephens, *Loners, Losers and Lovers.*

36   Ibid., p. 90.

37   Ibid., pp. 90-91.

38   Ibid., p. 91.

39   Ibid.

40   Ibid., p. 94.

41   Erlich, *St. Louis "Invisible" Elderly.*

42   Ibid., p. 9.

43   Ibid., p. 10.

44   Ibid.

45   Ibid., p. 11.

46   Shapiro, *Communities;* Siegal, *Outposts of the Forgotten;* Stephens, *Loners, Losers and Lovers.*

47   Erlich, *St. Louis "Invisible" Elderly;* T. Tissue, "Old Age, Poverty and the Central City," *Aging and Human Development,* 2 (1971).

48   Shapiro, *Communities;* Siegal, *Outposts of the Forgotten;* Stephens, *Loners, Losers and Lovers.*

49   Stephens, *Loners, Losers and Lovers,* p. 47.

50   Tissue, "Old Age, Poverty and the Inner City," p. 244.

51   Ibid.

52   Ibid., p. 245.

3

San Diego:
The Scene,
The Setting
and the Approach

San Diego, California, is the ninth largest city in the United States and the second largest city in California. In 1976, the city's population reached a total of 773,400. Distinctive ecological features of the San Diego area are its dry subtropical climate and proximity to the Pacific Ocean, the Laguna Mountains, and Tijuana in Baja California. San Diego has experienced rapid growth since the 1950s. This corresponds with the Korean War and San Diego's prominence as the headquarters for the Navy's Pacific Fleet.

With its excellent climate, San Diego is often thought to have a higher concentration of older persons than the average for the nation as a whole. However, as Erickson points out, San Diego does not have as old a population as is sometimes thought.[1] Instead, for both the United States and California, the census reports a median age of 28.1, in contrast to 25.6 for San Diego County (see Table 1).

Table 1

Average Age, Number and Percentage of Elderly by Race, For San Diego County, 1970°

	Median Age	Mean Age	No. of People 65+	% of People 65+
Blacks	20.9	24.5	2,183	3.5
Browns°°	20.6	24.7	6,442	3.7
Whites and Others	27.3	31.8	109,671	9.8
Total	25.6	30.6	118,296	8.7

° Table adapted from "Social Profiles of San Diego: Poverty and Race" Rosemary J. Erickson, Western Behavioral Sciences Institute, La Jolla, California, December, 1973.

°° Includes Spanish speaking or Spanish surname

The Research Setting: Census Tract 53

Census Tract 53 is located in the heart of downtown San Diego (Map A). The tract is divided evenly by Broadway, the main east-west transportation artery. Immediately evident is Broadway's function as a natural boundary dividing two worlds. North of Broadway underwent extensive urban renewal in the early 1960s. Within this new central business core are located newer constructions and fine hotels amid shops and parking lots. The area was improved to increase the sale potential of the center city, which had been losing ground to suburban shopping centers. The tallest building—twenty five stories—was built in 1966. A new civic center was created, with a spacious mall, an

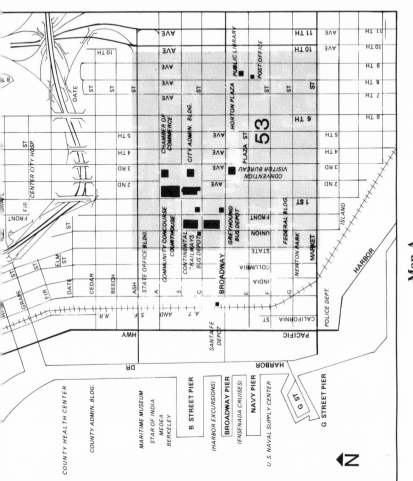

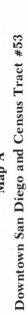

Map A

Downtown San Diego and Census Tract #53

opera house, meeting rooms, city offices and good parking facilities. The streets in this area are busy during the day with shoppers and business people; at night, they are quiet and deserted.

Broadway is also a boundary between the central business district to the north and the tenderloin to the south which, for the middle class has become "the other side of Broadway." Today, crossing Broadway involves a major change in the cultural tone of the environment. The streets are crowded with young and old both day and night. There are many pawn shops, massage parlors, dirty book stores, hard-core movie houses, cheap hotels, parking lots, bars, and a few new buildings. The streets and the sidewalks are less neatly kept than north of Broadway. Small groups of men loiter about talking or swigging on a bottle of wine inside a paper bag. Street action is continual; one is never alone regardless of the time of day. Thus, the census tract is in no way homogenous, but, instead an amalgam of two worlds easily separated by Broadway.

The econiches of "the other side of Broadway" are those of an area pretty far advanced in the decline phase of the rise and fall of neighborhoods. Such econiches have three dominating characteristics. First, they are cheap. Second, they have been thrust more or less out of sight of the more prosperous areas of citizens of the city. These two characteristics mean that two kinds of people are attracted to the area: those who are poor and those who have something to hide. Outsiders—and many of the media—fail to distinguish between the aged residents and other poor people of the area and those who are hiding something.

The third factor is that all the aspects of their culture that middle class people dislike (or claim to dislike) are pushed into this same hidden area. In the unseen crannies of cities can be found: the entire second-hand industry, major parts of the porno industry—dirty books and novelties, peep shows, "adult" movies, pimps and whores, transvestites and other sexual anomalies.

Thus, not only is the tenderloin associated with the poor and the hidden—it comes to be associated with the disapproved. In such hidden corners, all disapproved cultural pursuits come to be associated with poverty. As a result, all become "invisible," and when one set is flushed out, the others are not differentiated. In spite of this, it is important to remember that there are two sets of problems: those dealing with poor populations, including the elderly, and those dealing with social disorganization—drugs and alcoholism, pornography, prostitution, etc.

In 1973, Western Behavioral Sciences Institute (WBSI) conducted a social area analysis of San Diego County by census tract. The conceptual model used sought information on ethnic status, family status, and economic status for each census tract. In the 1970 census, tract 53 was the lowest in San Diego County on *family status*. The mean household size is 1.10, as compared to 2.86 nationally, and there were no child-rearing families in the tract.[2] The family status indicator points out that the lowest household sizes are found in the oldest parts of San Diego— these areas have the highest concentration of elderly. Census Tract 53 was third from the lowest in the county in *socioeconomic status* (a combination of the percentage of high school graduates twenty-five years and over and the value of the house or contact rent). Of unrelated individuals, 25.9 percent were below the poverty level, with a mean yearly income of $937. In addition, 33.8 percent were over sixty-five years of age.

Table 2, compiled by D'Arcy, illustrates a profile of population and percentages of persons age fifty-five and over based on the 1970 census. As she indicates, in 1970 persons fifty-five and over comprised almost half of the population in Tract 53. Of these persons, the majority were unrelated males.

More recent data based on a 1975 special census, conducted by the State Department of Finance for the County of San Diego, still indicates that the percentage of persons aged fifty-five and over exceeds the percentages for both the city and county. However, changes have occurred, especially in the percentage of persons sixty-five and over living in Tract 53—

there has been a marked decrease in the percentage of older persons. These figures take on added significance when contrasted with the percentage of persons twenty-five to twenty-nine years who have migrated into the area since 1970. In 1970, there were 441 persons in the twenty-five to twenty-nine year cohort, in 1975 the number increased to 1,157. These figures suggest that there is an in-migration of younger persons into the area and an out-migration of older persons (Table 3).

The portion of Census Tract 53 south of Broadway has long been considered San Diego's "Skid Row" cum "Tenderloin" area. As studies of other such areas have shown, women are in short supply.[3] In the area south of Broadway, men outnumber women almost four to one. This is partially due to the "seamy" nature of the area as well as the preference of women to keep their own house or apartment and do their own cooking. Even when they live in hotels, women often choose to clean their own room and sometimes voluntarily assist the maids in their chores.

This general demographic description of Census Tract 53 sets the stage for a closer look at the "skid row"/"tenderloin" area south of Broadway.

The Horton Plaza Redevelopment Project

Within the south-of-Broadway area are located three major redevelopment programs initiated by the City of San Diego to upgrade the area: the Horton Plaza Redevelopment Project, the Gaslamp Quarter, and Marina Redevelopment Project. The project having the most immediate significance for the area is the Horton Plaza Redevelopment Project initiated in 1972. This Project has progressed slowly. The major change in the forty acre redevelopment area has been the construction of a twenty-two story office building and federal courthouse complex. Other components of the project include a senior citizen tower to occupy the half block north of the Wells Fargo Hotel and a major retail complex. If the Horton Project is successful, it will result in the redevelopment of most properties

Table 2

Total Population and Percentages
of Persons Age 55 and Over

Population	U.S.A. (000)	%	CALIFORNIA (000)	%	County	%	SAN DIEGO City	%	Track 53	%
Total	203,166	100.0	20,296	100.0	1,357,854	100.0	696,769	100.0	3,618	100.0
Ages 55-64	15,600	7.7	1,704	8.4	103,482	7.6	52,659	7.6	462	12.8
65 and over	20,000	10.0	1,846	9.1	118,296	8.7	61,218	8.8	1,222	33.8
Total over 55	35,650	17.5	3,550	17.5	221,778	16.3	113,877	16.3	1,684	46.5

Source: U.S. Census of Population 1970. Compiled by A.M. D'Arcy, in "Elderly Hotel Residents and their Social Networks," Masters thesis. San Diego State University, 1976.

Table 3

Number and Percent Change in Select
Population Cohorts from 1970-1975

Age	1970	1975	Percent Change
75+	610	150	-75
65+	1,222	893	-27
55-64	462	328	-29
25-29	441	1,157	+162

Source: State Department of Finance, California, Special Census for the County of San Diego, 1975.

within the fifteen block area outlined. Some of the stated goals of the Horton Project follow:

> Provide an environment where a socially balanced community can work and live, by providing jobs and housing for persons of varying social, economic, and ethnic groups.

> Eliminate blighting influences, including incompatible and obnoxious land use, obsolete structures, congested streets, and inadequate parking facilities.

> Eliminate environmental deficiencies, including (among others) small and irregular lot and block subdivision, excessive streets and parking areas, *economic and social deficiencies,* and utilization of land and parking facilities.

> Upgrade the quality of life in the central area.

The Horton Project was expected to be completed over a ten-year period, but economic vissicitudes and difficulties in obtaining commitments from major retailers have slowed the project.

Hotels

D'Arcy has completed an excellent study of the social networks of elderly hotel residents in downtown San Diego.[4] As she noted, San Diego has a generous share of hotels—there are thirty in the downtown area. These hotels differ widely in function, size, and characteristics. Map B pinpoints the hotels and several important restaurants in the area one block north and four blocks south of Broadway in Census Tract 53.

Hotels tend to specialize in function. The larger higher class hotels specialize in transients staying for only a day or a week. Hotels in this category include the Sam Houston,

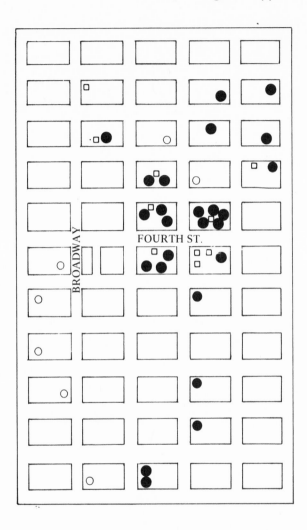

Map B

South of Broadway, with Hotels and Restaurants
Marked for Location Only
KEY:

● SRO Hotels
O Middle Class Commercial Hotel
□ Cheap Restaurants

American, Hanover House.° Some other hotels are a curious mixture of a transient and permanent clientele. For example, the Brunswick Hotel (250 rooms) adjoins the Greyhound Bus Station. It has moderate rates ($12-$14 for single room/night, $120-$150/month) and a busy transient clientele composed of recent arrivals to San Diego, sailors on weekend leave, and a larger older permanent group of residents. At least one-third of the rooms are occupied by older permanent residents. The William Tell is another hotel with a mixture of transients and permanent residents; however, it serves a largely homosexual clientele. The California Hotel, a specialty retirement hotel, caters to people fifty years and older who are ambulatory. It is the only hotel of its kind in the downtown area. It provides laundry facilities, meals, social and recreational activities to residents. Rooms (with board) vary in price from $140 to $249 per month (September 1974) depending on size, location, and bathroom arrangements.

Lower Rent Inner-City Hotels: The S.R.O.

Our major concern focuses on inexpensive hotels offering single furnished rooms suited to the incomes and needs of older persons on fixed incomes. These hotels have been popularly referred to as Single Room Occupancy (SRO) Hotels—the cheap hotels and rooming houses located in commercial areas adjacent to the downtown business district. The label, however, is misleading. In New York, where the label originated, SRO refers to slum apartment houses or welfare tenements converted into hotels for "socially terminal" persons of all ages and of predominantly minority ethnicity. These "tenement" hotels cater to a wide variety of residents and are viewed by scholars and public officials alike as the lowest form of housing available.

In San Diego the SRO hotel situation is quite different. Here we find structures designed as hotels, some specifically established to serve single working class men (Wells Fargo

---

° All names for hotels and people are fictitious.

Hotel). A large portion of the hotels were fashionable, if not fancy, in their day (Ballentine hotel, Majestic Hotel). What they have in common is a location in an area viewed as "blighted." The hotels vary widely in their state of repair and ratio of transients to permanent tenants. Most of the hotels in our purview cater to older, single, predominantly white males.

San Diego SRO hotels vary considerably in size, from 25 to 325 rooms, yet can be categorized along three lines: (1) Small walk-up hotels ranging from twenty-five to sixty-five rooms. These are usually located above pawn shops, dirty book stores, and cheap restaurants. They are usually without elevators and lobbies, never have private bathrooms attached to the rooms, seldom have telephones in the rooms, and are frequently in the worst repair. The managers often live on the premises—thus, we refer to them as Mom and Pop operations; (2) A second type of hotel ranges from 70-100 rooms. These hotels usually have lobbies on the ground floors, and in some cases, were higher class hotels in earlier days. Their condition is deteriorating, yet they still maintain formal services such as linen, maid, and telephones in rooms. These hotels usually have elevators as well as T.V. viewing rooms. They contain several types of rooms. Some portions are available with private baths and televisions. Prices also vary according to whether the room is "outside" (facing the street) or "inside" (no view of the street—facing an interior court or air shaft). State of hotel repair varies from average to poor; (3) Larger size is the major feature distinguishing the last type of hotel. These are large operations ranging from 250-325 rooms. They tend to be well run and better maintained than the smaller hotels. Hotel management and staff are better paid, therefore more stable, dependable and professional. Without exception they offer maid, linen, and telephone services. All have lobbies and T.V. viewing rooms.

These hotels also vary on the basis of the typical groups to which they cater. Some have strict policies about drinking while others cater to alcoholics; some cater to a younger clientele while others prefer retirees.

There are other features common to these hotels. A

large proportion of the hotel rooms are without baths. Toilet facilities and showers are usually provided on each floor—larger hotels provide separate facilities for each sex. Hotels vary in allowing double occupancy. Some permit only single room occupancy, others will make adjustments if double occupancy is required. The hotels usually have rules governing how long visitors may stay "upstairs." The Ballentine Hotel formally states that the decision to have visitors rests with the desk clerk on duty. This is the case in most hotels regardless of formal rulings. The hotels usually lack kitchens. Formal rulings forbid hot plates or other appliances for cooking. This rule is almost universally abused—a large proportion of residents have at least a hot plate for heating water or soup. Single room occupancy hotels have at least half of their tenants living there on a permanent basis (defined as six months or more). All SRO hotels are commercial establishments and not licensed or subsidized for institutional care. Communal television rooms are provided in the La Bar, Wells Fargo, La Salle, General Lee and Ballentine hotels. The Ballentine and Wells Fargo hotels provide laundry facilities.

The price of rooms varies widely among and within the hotels. They range from approximately $65 to $150 per month. For example, at the Wells Fargo Hotel one can rent a small room without bath (dimension 8' x 11') for $65. At the same hotel one can rent a room twice the size with bath for $150/month. A similar situation exists at the Ballentine and some other larger hotels. The most commonly quoted price for a room is between $65 and 75 a month. As D'Arcy points out, the physical condition or appearance of a hotel, or location north or south of Broadway, has little influence on price.[5] For example, rooms with bath at the Brunswick Hotel range from $120-$140/month, $10-$30/month less expensive than comparable rooms at the Wells Fargo or Ballentine hotels.

The Wells Fargo Hotel - The largest, best known, and oldest of the cheaper hotels south of Broadway is the Wells Fargo. The Wells Fargo Hotel is situated in the heart of the skid row cum tenderloin area, between Third and Fourth Avenue on "G" Street (shown on map). Opened on December 1, 1913, it was built to provide "simple, inexpensive accommodations" for working men. Rooms in 1976 rented for $70 to $156 per month.

John Lloyd Wright designed the hotel, shortly before joining his father, Frank Lloyd Wright, to initiate work on the Imperial Hotel in Tokyo. He relied heavily on the principles of the Chicago school of American architecture, and the result is a strong, somewhat austere concrete building. It is totally fireproof, with the only structural wood being found in the doors, door frames, and window frames. Each of the three floors in the building contains communal bathrooms with showers and tubs.

Few changes have been made to the hotel since 1913, although a few years ago seventy-five of the rooms were enlarged. However, the resident population of the hotel has changed dramatically over the years. From its original population of "working" men, the population has shifted to nonworking, marginally subsistent pensioners. The total resident population is more than 300. According to the manager, the average age of the residents is "around seventy" and over two-thirds of them are pensioners (recipients of Social Security, disability pensions, or welfare). The manager estimates that the average income of the residents is somewhere between $200 and $250 per month, and the ethnographic information agrees. Seventy-five percent of the residents are "permanent." The rest are "transients." Only twenty of the residents are female. The hotel has sometimes been used as a first shelter placement for paroled ex-offenders, but their numbers are small. It also serves a small but increasing subpopulation of young persons, most of whom have an ambulatory physical disability and have been placed in the Wells Fargo by relatives as social/health agencies for quasi-custodial purposes.

Compared with other hotels catering to the indigent (such as those described by Bogue,[6] the Wells Fargo is relatively clean, organized, and comfortable. There are twenty-four full-time employees working in the hotel, all rooms have curtains, the linen is changed every week, with maid service five times a week. The manager and staff profess to "look out after the old guys." Bogue notes that residents of such hotels have very definite ideas about the kind of housing they prefer.

> They are almost unanimously opposed to cubicle hotels and open dormitories. Instead, they aspire to single rooms (even if very simply built and austerely furnished), or to one-man efficiency apartments where they can prepare their own meals. They do not want to share their quarters with other men, but prefer to live alone. This pattern characterizes elderly men, working men, and heavy drinkers alike.[7]

The skid row men studied by Bogue also noted the importance of considerate, kind, and understanding hotel staff.[8] It can readily be seen that the Wells Fargo Hotel is not a rundown, filthy "flop-house" catering to skid row alcoholic transients. Though a few of the residents are alcoholics, the Wells Fargo primarily contains marginally subsistent aged individuals, whose lives are fairly stable and whose basic needs are minimally satisfied.

The Ballentine Hotel - The Ballentine Hotel is somewhat smaller than the Wells Fargo Hotel—ninety-five rooms—and charges higher rates. Approximately 70 percent of the residents are permanents—mostly marginally subsistent elderly on fixed incomes. Some of the permanents have lived at the Ballentine for over twenty-two years. The smaller size of the Ballentine contributes to a more intimate social climate than that found in the Wells Fargo. There is an active transient clientele at the Ballentine made up mostly of sailors, pimps and prostitutes, as well as persons who work in the local restaurants, bars, bookstores and theatres. The Horton Redevelopment Project has slated the Ballentine for demolition in 1980 and its ever-deteriorating state is of concern to the residents.

The Ballentine was constructed in 1923 and served as a middle-class hostelry until the 1930s. During its heyday, performers from the adjacent Balboa Theatre would lodge there. During the Second World War, the hotel was active as a residential center and had a low vacancy rate. Since that time the hotel has gone through numerous owners and has deteriorated slowly.

Maid and laundry service at the Ballentine is sporadic. The professed poor economic status of the hotel keeps salaries low ($2.00/hr.) and contributes to high employee turnover. The lobby of the hotel has several couches and chairs; there is a separate T.V. room.

South of Broadway: San Diego's "Skid Row"

Robert Redfield's ecological approach helps in understanding San Diego's cheap hotels and urban milieu.[9] Redfield concentrated on the small community as an integrated whole capable of systematic description. In the small village communities of the Yucatan Peninsula, Redfield began to see that the activities of the Indians were in part reflections of the regularities and irregularities of nature. The ecological system defined the community and its cyclical patterning.

In the urban context, however, the interrelationships between man and nature are minimized,

> In the human ecology of American society it becomes a study of the spatial and temporal orders of settlement and of institutions without much reference to animals, plants, and the weather.[10]

As Redfield points out, the Indians had little control over the exigencies of nature. Similarly, the older residents and other powerless persons living in cheap hotels have little control over the actions of planners and others who view the area negatively. The forces defining and exerting control over major parts of the "skid row" area are located out of the community and in many cases are not publicly known. The neighborhood is distinct in symbolic terms—it is a "skid row" or "zone of deterioration."

Overall, the area south of Broadway meets the classic description of a "skid row."[11] It has a preponderance of substandard hotels for single men. The hotels charge low rents that "fit" the minimal fixed incomes of the male clientele. The hotels are intermingled with numerous restaurants serving low cost meals, taverns, pawnshops, secondhand book stores, and missions that provide meals after the services. In addition, there are barber colleges, burlesque shows and nightclubs with topless dancers, massage parlors, penny arcades, card rooms, tattoo parlors, bakeries selling stale bread, warehouses, parking lots, and thrift shops selling used clothing and appliances. The area is located near storehouses, the freight yards and waterfront, empty lots and vacant buildings.

Researchers have tended to define skid row as a specific subcultural community with a distinct and recognizable way of life.[12] In particular, Blumberg, Shipley and Moer emphasize the integration of skid row with other parts of the city and the similarity of its people with those living elsewhere. They point to the similarity of skid row people to other powerless people living in metropolitan areas. They view skid row not so much as a place as a human condition characterized by minimal income, life outside "normal" family relationships, low-cost housing, altercations with police resulting from alcohol use and other "deviant" behaviors, susceptibility to victimization, superficial social relations, and a prognosis for continued low status or even downward mobility.[13]

The approaches to skid row as (1) a geographic place coordinated with space and time or, more recently, as (2) a human condition, are not mutually exclusive; both are helpful. The perspective of a skid row area sensitizes us to special ecological characteristics not readily found in other urban residential zones. It provides us with a view of context, a context of different symbolic nature and population composition.

Jennie-Keith Ross suggests that three themes consistently appear in the voluminous literature discussing community: territory, we-feeling, and social organization.[14] These three components join together to form a composite definition in which territory can be delimited and we-feelings and patterned organization of social life can be evaluated as being present to a lesser or greater extent. Ross states that:

"the higher the overall level of these characteristics, including the presence of territory, the greater degree to which community is present."[15]

Viewed in these terms the south of Broadway area and the SRO hotels within it meet the minimal criteria of a community. In terms of territory, the general area south of Broadway is distinct both geographically and symbolically. It is characterized as a deteriorated zone with many social problems.

Within the hotels themselves, a sense of we-ness emerges among older residents of similar background, age, and economic status. The primary forces uniting these older residents are the shared values of self-reliance and independence as well as the behavioral norms demanding that people should mind their own business and maintain personal autonomy. As an environment demanding very little social participation, individuals who resist intimacy are bound to each other by their common desire to avoid closeness to anyone. Other features uniting residents are common needs, interests, threats to their safety, and other common problems. We-feeling is further exemplified in the way residents look at their own social world in contrast to the negative viewpoint held by outsiders. A common indication of we-feeling is the frequent reply made by older hotel residents when asked why they live in south of Broadway hotels. They say, "I feel comfortable here, I'm among my own kind."

The third criterion of community concerns social organization. Social organization includes the social patterns and identifiable roles and expectations which help to define boundaries between various groups. In the SRO hotels social patterning of behavior is discernable though minimal. The behavior and mutual expectations of the older residents vis-a-vis hotel managers and staff, young transients, helping professionals, and among themselves are regular enough to provide for the formation of the SRO social world and community. Unlike retirement communities, the hotels lack formal organizations and organized social activities.

Participant Observation and the Personal Approach

Pelto and Pelto point out that ethnographic methodology after Malinowski has become more and more oriented to what can be called "community study."[16] Such research tends toward holistic, qualitative descriptions of life in non-Western face-to-face communities.

The ethnographic approach has been equally important in sociological research focusing on industrialized urban cultures. Urban ethnography is rooted in the early work of Robert Park and other sociologists at the University of Chicago. As Suttles suggests, some scholars date the real beginning of urban ethnography with the establishment of the "Chicago School."[17] Some of the best known ethnographies emanating from the Chicago researchers include: Zorbaugh's *The Gold Coast and the Slum* (1929), Shaw's *The Jack Roller* (1930), Whyte's *Street Corner Society* (1943).[18]

The tradition of urban ethnography has continued to the present day, with the 1960s spawning several excellent studies such as Gans's *Urban Villagers,* Liebow's *Tally's Corner,* and Hannerz's *Soulside: Inquiries into Ghetto Culture and Community.*[19]

Several important factors support the use of an ethnographic approach in studies of urban communities. First, many urban ethnographers have tended to study groups whose behavior has been little understood and labeled as deviant, irrational or aberrant by the dominant culture. Ethnographic approaches are sensitive to discovering the ways in which members of specific groups view their appearance, thus overcoming "outsiders" definitions and viewpoints—their task is to discover the "insiders" point of view. Additionally, ethnographic approaches using an eclectic mixture of methods overcome the inherent weakness of single methodologies. For example, several researchers[20] have pointed to the suspicion that persons deemed to be "lower-class" are less tractable to interview and questionnaire techniques than are persons in the middle and upper strata. Therefore, broad ethnographic approaches utilizing participant observation and other methods give the best assurance that data will accurately reflect the insider's perceptions and behaviors.

Field Methods

Participant observation has been the modus operandi in the study of older hotel residents. Residence was maintained in the downtown area from September, 1975 to September, 1976. I rented a room in one hotel (the Brunswick) for the entire year. However, I lived and worked in another hotel (the Ballentine) from January until April of 1976.*

The initial phase of research in SRO hotels involved *direct observation* of the behavior of local residents in a variety of situations—hotels, hotel lobbies, restaurants, buses, parks. The basic assumption was that the subtleties of hotel life could only be gained through total immersion in the hotel milieu. Living in the hotel allowed me to observe dramatic events (e.g., hotel fires) that could not be anticipated in advance. For the occasional observer, such events often pass with little notice in the quick paced and often impersonal urban scene. For example, knowledge of a death in the hotel might constitute a passing remark of a resident or desk clerk. Evidence of a fire might be known only by the burnt mattress on the curb awaiting disposal. Retrospective inquiries often fail to convey what really happened during an incident.

Early on, much time was spent in local restaurants and other places used by older hotel residents. Many mornings were spent sitting in hotel lobbies and local restaurants listening and talking to residents as they passed the time. Such sessions were useful in discovering the community facilities utilized by residents in the area. Buses and bus stop benches provided a setting for discussions with older downtown residents. Casual encounters frequently developed into an opportunity to buy someone a cup of coffee and continue conversation.

In situations in which conversation progressed beyond preliminary exchanges, the rule was to present myself as a research associate with the Western Behavioral Sciences Institute, explain the nature of the Unseen Community Study, and the intent to write a book about the area and its inhabitants. Persons listened patiently as I described my purposes, but seldom asked questions or showed interest in obtaining additional information. After persons determined that I was a "good guy" (often determined on the basis of being a good listener) they would open up and talk freely. Empathy, genuine caring, and understanding were key factors in establishing rapport with persons contacted in the study. Several respondents reported that they valued these qualities.

Interviewing persons was avoided on days where I felt emotionally drained or discouraged with my progress—I learned to "take off" at such times. My intent was to live by the same pattern I was observing in others. On many days, I would go to breakfast around 8:00 a.m. to 10:00 a.m., sit and talk with individuals (waitresses and regulars), return to the hotel lobby, sit around and talk, go for dinner in mid-afternoon, then take a walk or sit in Horton Plaza. Evenings were spent on the street, in the hotel lobby, or in my room. This pattern with variations was routine for a number of the persons with whom I became acquainted. At other times, I rearranged my sleeping patterns to correspond to those who slept during the day and participated in the late night scene—a pattern not typical of older residents. Few older residents were active in the late night bar scene. However, some spent many late nights awake sitting alone in the lobby, chatting with the desk clerk or other persons unable to sleep.

The role of *participant-as-observer* was deemed the appropriate initial stance for data collection. It was obvious that the role of complete participant was not feasible, because of age differences and the lack of interaction between transient and permanent hotel residents. Transients were often viewed with suspicion and avoided by permanent residents of the hotels. This initial handicap was partially overcome by assuming the role of researcher studying the renewal area and its residents. Since my monthly stipend check was equal to the average monthly income of persons in the hotel sample population, I worked out a budget and tried to live within the economic limits experienced by older residents. The role of "marginal native" provided flexibility and allowed relatively free movement among different sectors of the social system. In the Brunswick, main channels of social relationships developed along two lines: (1) the family of the hotel owner living in an apartment in the hotel; (2) a group of older male permanent hotel residents referred to by some as the "lobby lizards." This group of residents had lived in the hotel for years and considered it home. They were on a first name basis with the hotel management and employees.

Data gathered through informal and unstructured interviews were recorded descriptively after encounters. To aid in recall, notes and key phrases were recorded in a small notebook as soon as possible. Informal interviews were not taped, and I never felt comfortable in taking notes in public places during informal discussions. Great care was taken to avoid an "official" image that would label me as a "vice," "narc," "social worker," or other type commonly associated with "the establishment." Later, in my room, detailed notes were recorded in a daily log which included ongoing observations, conversations, interviews, self-reflections and tentative analyses.

During the second phase of participant observation (from January to April), I was able to participate directly in the life of the study group. In *direct participation*, the investigator assumes a role within the study group and becomes involved in day-to-day activities. This opportunity occurred when I was hired as relief desk clerk at the Ballentine Hotel. As desk clerk, I was able to observe the tasks involved in management of the hotel, hotel managers' and employees' perceptions of their jobs and the residents, and their modes of control and support. In short, working "behind the desk" thrust me into the normal flow of hotel social transactions. In the desk clerk role I was able to establish relationships with several long-term hotel residents as well as to become acquainted with all the employees of the

hotel. In this position I was able to observe, assess, and participate in transactions with the police, vice squad, community
mental health workers, and other social service personnel.
Additionally, it allowed me firsthand contact and experience
with the many different types of persons using the south-of-
Broadway turf. These various kinds of participation in the life of
the SRO hotel residents allowed me to observe aspects of the
hotel social structure and organization that would have been
lost through use of nonparticipating methodologies.

Conceptualizing the community in transactional terms
necessitated adherence to methodologies adequate to
describing relationships not restrained by common boundaries.
Social network analysis[21] provided an approach for defining the
social relationships between individuals bound together through
common needs and interests. Social network analysis centers on
the individual as the central node in all social relationships:

> Each person is, as it were, in touch with a number of people,
> some of whom are directly in touch with each other and some
> who are not . . . I find it convenient to talk of a social field of
> this kind as a network. The image I have is of a set of points,
> some of which are joined by lines. The points of the image are
> people, and sometimes groups, and the lines indicate which
> people interact with each other.[22]

Sensitivity to social network theory proved useful in
understanding the interrelationships between older hotel
residents and the persons with whom they interact as well as
their individual adjustments to the hotel setting.

The hotel manager was moderately supportive of my
research but more interested in the simple fact that I was a
dependable, enthusiastic employee. Working as the "relief"
clerk necessitated that I learn the various tasks associated with
each shift. I quickly learned the demands of each shift and
convinced the manager of my capabilities. My status as student
working toward the Ph.D. was viewed positively. The manager
would often introduce me to people as a student working on my
doctorate. At one time in his past, he had had educational
aspirations and attended a theological seminary. Although his

plans were never realized, he identified with my commitment to education.

Several anthropologists writing on ethnographic methodology have called for multimethodological approaches—traditional methods and standardized procedures.[23] Supplementing participant observation as the basic research technique this study benefited from several research methods including survey questionnaires, random sampling, and life history interviews.

Random sample analysis of persons fifty years old and over in twelve hotels of various types aided in understanding the lives of the older person beyond the confines of an individual hotel. The hotels where SRO elderly lived represented a continuum ranging from lower middle-class to "skid-row." In this way, researcher bias was partially overcome in the selection of possible respondents and informants. Further insight and information on the area and residents was gained from numerous groups, including police, cafe owners and waitresses, service personnel (rescue missions, salvation army, preachers), social workers, novelty shop employees, barber college persons, city employees, students.

Field-worker observations were assisted through membership in a multiperson field team. My association with Western Behavioral Science Institute (WBSI) allowed me to participate in a setting where multiple as opposed to single observers were employed. Regular debriefing sessions held by Paul Bohannan, Principal Investigator for the WBSI study, and Anthony Gorman, a WBSI field-worker who was living in the Wells Fargo Hotel, allowed comparison of notes and observations. I was able to participate in these sessions for the duration of my field research. The use and interaction of multiple observers helped to remove potential bias introduced by lone field-workers. The sessions aided in pinpointing further areas of observation and inquiry. Independent reporting of the same kinds of observations and personal perspectives without prior consultation increased confidence and reliability. On occasion, sessions took the form of a field methods training seminar where individual problems could be discussed and solutions offered. I found the sessions a boost to my morale, especially when colleagues were able to corroborate an observation.

Other methods included a limited number of life history interviews, an extensive photographic record, and a variety of unobtrusive measures (analysis of hotel records, physical trace analysis, simple observation). In addition, daily diaries, life history interviews, and debriefing notes from the larger WBSI study were available for comparative purposes.

A continual topic of conversation and matter of concern for older hotel residents was their state of health. Since health emerged as a central theme in the lives of the older residents, I decided to conduct a medically oriented substudy focused on their mental and physical health status and issues related to health care utilization. The health substudy is the subject of Chapter 10.

With the scene and setting described and the overall methodological approach outlined, the next chapter gives an ethnographic portrait of one SRO hotel and its residents.

Notes

1   R.J. Erickson, *Social Profiles of San Diego:* I. *A Social Area Analysis* (La Jolla, Ca.: Western Behavioral Sciences Institute, 1973).

2   United States Department of Commerce, Bureau of the Census, *Statistical Abstract of the United States,* 99th Annual Edition (Washington, D.C.: U.S. Government Printing Office, 1978).

3   D.J. Bogue, *Skid-row in American Cities.* (Chicago: University and Family Study Center, 1963); T. Caplow et al., *A General Report on the Problem of Relocating the Population of the Lower Loop Redevelopment Area.* Multilith (Minneapolis: Minneapolis Housing and Redevelopment Authority).

4   A.M. D'Arcy, "Elderly Hotel Residents and Their Social Networks in Downtown San Diego," Masters thesis, San Diego State University, 1976.

5   Ibid.

6   Bogue, *Skid-row*.

7   Ibid. p. 449.

8   Ibid., pp. 493-94.

9   R. Redfield, *The Little Community* (Chicago: University of Chicago Press, 1953).

10   Ibid., p. 29.

11   Bogue, *Skid-row*, p. 1.

12   S.E. Wallace, *Skid Row as a Way of Life* (Totowa, N.J.: Bedminister Press, 1963); L. Blumberg, T.E. Shipley, Jr. and J.O. Moor, "The Skid Row Man and the Skid Row Status Community." *Quarterly Journal of Studies on Alcohol*, 32 (1971):909-41.

13   Ibid.

14   J.K. Ross, *Old People, New Lives (Community Creation in a Retirement Residence)* (Chicago: University of Chicago Press, 1977), p. 5.

15   Ibid., p. 6.

16   P.J. Pelto and G. Pelto, "Ethnography: The Fieldwork Enterprise," in *Handbook of Social and Cultural Anthropology*, ed. J.J. Honigmann (Chicago: Rand McNally, 1973), p. 244.

17   G.D. Suttles, "Urban Ethnography: Situational and Normative Accounts," in *Annual Review of Sociology*, ed. A. Inkeles, J. Coleman and N. Smelser, vol. 2 (Palo Alto: Annual Review, Inc.).

18   H.W. Zorbaugh, *The Golden Coast and the Slums* (Chicago: University of Chicago Press, 1926); C. Shaw, *The Jack Roller: A Delinquent Boy's Own Story* (Chicago: University of Chicago Press, 1930); W.F. Whyte, *Street Corner Society: The Social Structure of an Italian Slum* (Chicago: University of Chicago Press, 1943).

19   H. Gans, The Urban Villagers (New York: Free Press, 1962); E. Liebow, *Tally's Corner* (Boston: Little, Brown, 1967); U. Hannerz, *Soulside: Inquiries into Ghetto Culture and Community* (New York: Columbia University Press, 1969).

20   A.K. Cohen and H. Hodges, "Characteristics of the Lower Blue-Collar Class," *Social Problems*, 10, no. 4 (1963): 333; S.M. Miller and F. Riessman, "The Working Class Subculture: A New View," *Social Problems*, 9, no. 1 (1961):92; Liebow, *Tally's Corner*, p. 9.

21   E. Bott, *Family and Social Networks* (London: Tavistock Publications, 1957). J. Boissevain, "The Place of Non-groups in the Social Sciences," *Man* (N.S.), 3 (1968); J. Boissevain, *Friend of Friends: Networks, Manipulators, and Coalitions* (Oxford: Basil Blackwell, 1974); A.L. Epstein, "Gossips, Norms, and Social Networks," in *Social Networks in Urban Situations*, ed. J. Clyde Mitchell (Manchester: Manchester University Press, 1969).

22   Bott, *Family and Social Networks* p. 34.

23   G. Berreman, "Ethnography: Method and Product," in *Introduction to Cultural Anthropology*, ed. James Clifton (Boston: Houghton-Mifflin, 1968); R. Cohen, "Generalization in Ethnology," in *A Handbook of Method in Cultural Anthropology*, ed. Raoul Naroll and Ronald Cohen (Garden City: Natural History Press, 1970); J.J. Honigman, "The Personal Approach in Cultural Anthropology Research," *Current Anthropology*, 17, no. 2 (June, 1976): 243-61; Pelto and Pelto, "Ethnography."

4

A Medium-Size SRO Hotel:
The Ballentine

From January until April of 1976, I lived and worked as a desk clerk in the Ballentine Hotel. Initially, the Ballentine seemed to be a transient hotel catering predominantly to younger alcoholic males on welfare. In the course of several months of fieldwork it became increasingly clear that the Ballentine's fairly large proportion (60 percent) of older residents on minimal fixed incomes was its backbone. I lived at the hotel for two weeks before being offered a job as a desk clerk. This factor (coupled with the large percentage of older residents) aided in the selection of the Ballentine as the primary hotel for ethnographic consideration. Since ethnographic information was collected on other hotels as well, comparisons will be made wherever they are appropriate.

The Ballentine is smaller and charges slightly higher rents ($80 to $150 per month) than the Wells Fargo Hotel described briefly in Chapter 3. Despite residents' awareness of the hotel's deteriorating condition, they consider it better than most of the hotels south of Broadway. Likewise, most residents of the other hotels believe their hotel to be a little nicer than the next. Residents who have lived in the hotel for some years frequently reminisce about what a "nice hotel this was before the new owners took over."

The Ballentine is one in a chain of five hotels—all located south of Broadway. Each hotel has a separate manager and caters to a slightly different clientele. The Balboa Hotel is considered middle class and charges higher rents ($120 to over $210 per month). Approximately 40 percent of the residents are retirees living there on a permanent basis. Another hotel in the chain caters to male homosexuals and has few older permanent residents. All of the five hotels are under the control of a general manager stationed in the Balboa Hotel. It is rumored that the entire operation is owned by a land speculator living in another city.

The residents, desk clerks, and the manager at the Ballentine all have complaints about the general manager. The residents feel that under the present owner, general manager, and manager, the hotel is being allowed to deteriorate at a rapid rate. They see little money going into the hotel for paint, carpeting, and necessary repairs, yet the rent continues to increase. Additionally, cutbacks in hotel staff mean that residents get fewer services. They also see hotel policies changing in favor of a larger percentage of transient clientele comprised both of pimps and prostitutes and of sailors on weekend shore leave.

The manager of the Ballentine shares some of the residents' concerns. For him, managing the hotel is a balancing act between the general manager's demands and the needs and wishes of the tenants. His major problem is how to keep the hotel staffed and operating. Permitted to pay salaries of only $2° per hour, he cannot be selective about whom he employs. Next comes the problem of keeping residents reasonably quiet—in his own words, "off my back." In order to achieve this, he sees that minimal repairs are made. Bathrooms, showers, the elevator, and the heat (in the winter) are kept in operation. He makes an effort to do his best. Wherever it is possible, he attributes his problems to the owner's and the general manager's austerity program.

Many of the SRO hotels are old, deteriorated, and ultimately a target for urban renewal. Therefore, the real value

All indications of salaries and expenses refer to conditions as of 1976.

of owning such hotels is the value of the land. Until the "redevelopment" of the area is an actuality, owners hope to get what money they can from them. Thus, little is invested in the physical plant—the hotels are "milked" for all that can be gotten out of them.

The Ballentine's four floors present an unassuming facade. On the ground level, the hotel houses several small businesses—a barber shop, card room, topless discotheque, cigar and newspaper shop, and a religious organization. Several of the office spaces are vacant, reflecting the marginal status and high turnover of small businesses in the area. There are two low-rent skid-row-type hotels on the same block; each houses a large percentage of permanent residents (over 50 percent having lived there for more than six months). Most of the permanent residents are single males.

One of the other hotels on the block, the General Lee, belongs to the same chain as the Ballentine. This hotels caters to a predominantly alcoholic clientele and charges lower rent than the Ballentine. Customers who appear drunk or questionable to the desk clerks at the Ballentine are frequently referred to the General Lee Hotel. On the same block with the Ballentine are several cheap restaurants (one offering a food delivery service), two pornographic theatres, a pawnshop, a tattoo parlor, barber shop, card room, and parking lot. Street action is continual, day and night. Sailors on shore leave walk slowly or hang on corners; pimps and prostitutes are plying their trade; older retirees take walks; small groups of loitering men talk or swig on a bottle of wine hidden inside a paper sack. This block is typical of many others in the area south of Broadway.

The block just northwest of the Ballentine is an exception to others south of Broadway. There sits a recently completed twenty-two story office building. Only three floors of the building are occupied, underlining the fact that there is much available office space in the downtown. Surrounding the new office building is a pedestrian area with a few benches, a sculpture, and several planters with trees. The open space is used by only a few individuals—mostly middle-class office workers taking lunch at the fast food restaurant on the ground level of the building. Older persons and others frequently referred to by the media as the "seamy element" are curiously absent. For them, the action is just across the street at the Horton Plaza—a small park with a fountain, grass, benches, and people of all ages, race, and classes.

Unlike some of the smaller "walk up" hotels, the Ballentine has a small but comfortable lobby and T.V. room.[1] The lobby is furnished in several comfortable chairs and sofas, a few lamps, and sand buckets for cigarettes. The positioning of the chairs and sofas along either side of the lobby allows for a view of the street and the passing of people in and out of the hotel. The spacing between the sofas and chairs is not conducive to conversation; instead, it almost demands privacy. If individuals choose to converse, they share a sofa. The hotel "desk" forms a semi-circle in one corner at the rear of the lobby; behind it is the manager's office and a storeroom. From the desk, the clerk is able to see the front and side entrances to the lobby, activities in the lobby and T.V. room, the elevator, and the stairway.

The T.V. room, separate from the lobby, is in constant use from mid-morning until late night hours. It seats approximately a dozen persons. Located in the T.V. room are three vending machines offering cigarettes, sodas, coffee, tea, soup, hot chocolate, peanuts, cookies, and some other snacks. There is also a locked restroom (the key is kept by the desk clerk) and public telephone on the ground floor. In the basement is a coin-operated washer and dryer.

Whether a hotel has an elevator is an important criterion when older persons limited in their mobility select a place to live. The elevator in the Ballentine is of the predepression manual variety. In an effort to save money, the elevator operator had been layed off long ago. The desk clerk is responsible for operating the elevator and the telephone switchboard, as well as checking persons in and out of the hotel. Multiple demands mean that the front desk and switchboard are left unattended when the elevator is in use. There is little hotel security when the desk clerk is operating the elevator. While working as a clerk, I discovered that persons desiring access to the upper floors of the hotel would wait outside the hotel until they saw me enter the elevator then dash into the hotel and up the stairs. Some residents feeling frustrated by the elevator situation hesitate to ask the clerks to take them upstairs. They wait in the lobby until someone else rings the buzzer to go up or come down. Some residents become impatient if the clerks are busy and do not respond immediately to their calls. Two residents, unable to walk up and down stairs, rely exclusively on the elevator and become captive to their room and floor when it is out of order (on the average, four days a month).

Approximately thirty-one rooms are located on each of the three upper floors. The majority of the rooms on the second floor are reserved for transient guests; they command higher rents ($12.00/15.00 per night, or $45.00 per week). These rooms have newer furnishings, window drapes, and color television sets. Some have private baths, but the majority do not. Rooms without bath have a wash basin with running water. Each floor has public restrooms and showers (one for men and one for women). The second floor hallway is better lit and less deteriorated than either the third or fourth floor hallways.

The permanent residents occupy most of the rooms on the third and fourth floors. The hallways are poorly lit, the walls grimy, and the carpeting soiled and torn. While much of the deterioration is of a superficial nature, some things create real threats for residents. For example, after having near-falls, several residents complained about the torn carpeting in the hallways and on the stairs. One older resident fell and broke her arm. The management paid all her medical bills and gave her six months free rent, yet failed to repair the carpet for several more months. Extensive water damage is evident in the hallways from activation of the overhead sprinkler system during previous fires.

Rooms on the third and fourth floors are cheaper, but in the worst repair. Some have been occupied by the same tenants for more than ten years. In a few cases, tenants personalize their rooms with a colorful bedspread or comfortable chair and one woman kept plants on her window sill. In general, however, the residents do not personalize their rooms. This is no surprise, since most tenants have so few personal possessions (those that do would not risk keeping them in their rooms). In most cases, a person's belongings amount to what can be packed in a suitcase, box, or paper sack.

A typical room is sparsely furnished with a marsh-mallow-mattressed bed and worn spread, used dresser with missing knobs, a straightback chair, and used desk. Lighting consists of a single 100-watt light bulb in a ceiling fixture. In the room I rented, the carpeting and walls were very soiled. The wash basin was foul smelling and had been used for micturation. The room had a definite smell created by wash basin odors combined with layered dirt, grime, and wax on old furniture. I also discovered that the door latch could be opened with a plastic credit card. Heat in the room (in winter, the temperatures at night in San Diego range from 40-50 degrees) was supplied by a loud hot water radiator which supplied either too much heat or none at all. A typical room at the Ballentine measures nine by fifteen feet and is larger than rooms in some other hotels (a common complaint made by residents at the Wells Fargo was that the rooms were too small—only eight by eleven feet). All rooms at the Ballentine have windows, though some face a narrow air space between buildings. Many of the transoms have been nailed shut by tenants to increase their security.

Security is an ever-present concern for older residents. On that subject they are most critical of the management. They view the lack of an elevator operator as not only a personal inconvenience, but one that may jeopardize their safety. When the desk is left unattended, they comment that any "crazy" can "walk right upstairs." When upstairs, they can break into rooms, mug someone in the hallways, or burn down the hotel. To combat their vulnerability, some residents take it upon themselves to watch the lobby while the clerks are attending to other business.

In addition, the high turnover of hotel staff creates its own security problems. At their wages per hour, few of the staff feel a commitment to the hotel or to their jobs. The continual succession of new faces makes residents suspicious—thus, some residents will not allow new maids into their rooms for housekeeping services. As one clerk reported to me, "A lot of the good maids work here a short time, then go elsewhere. They can get as much as $.60 an hour more at other hotels." In spite of these concerns, residents report that they feel safe inside their rooms.

The first month I lived in the Ballentine, there were three fires. Arson was suspected in the two cases in which the rooms were vacant. Rumor had it that unknown persons had entered the hotel when the desk was unattended, gone upstairs and flicked lighted matches or cigarettes through open transoms. Another rumor was that the night clerk had been allowing prostitutes to use the rooms and had not reported them as rented, and the temporary occupants had dropped lit cigarettes on the floor or mattress. I witnessed one incident in which an employee was laid off and, in anger, threatened to "burn the place down."

In the Ballentine, as in other hotels south of Broadway, it is common for tenants to have a hot plate for warming canned soup or heating water for coffee. In one case, a tenant had a refrigerator, toaster oven, and coffee pot crammed into a corner of his room. While official hotel policy prohibits cooking in rooms, there is no effort to enforce this policy. The Ballentine, like all other hotels in the downtown, is roach infested. However, unlike New York City's single-room-occupancy hotels and rooming houses, San Diego's hotels are free of rats.

There is considerable similarity in appearance among the twelve hotels I know something about. There is an overall drabness and lack of color in all of them. At most of the hotels, attempts are made to keep hallways free of trash and the bathrooms usable. At the Ballentine, hygenic conditions of the public bathrooms vary greatly. Since the hotel is severely understaffed, a stopped toilet or clogged shower drain may remain out of order for a day or two. One maintenance man is responsible for the five hotels in the chain. Since all the buildings are old and in need of continual maintenance, there is little opportunity for restorative maintenance.[2]

The hotels south of Broadway provide an almost entirely male environment. At the Wells Fargo Hotel, for example, the population is nearly 100 percent male. At the Ballentine, however, approximately 15 percent of the permanent residents are women. Some of the younger women residing permanently in the hotel work as waitresses, hotel desk clerks, bar maids, and dancers. Younger employed men residing premanently at the Ballentine work in the downtown area in the small businesses, card rooms, bars, and theatres.

Interspersed with the older tenants are transients of all ages, alcoholics (usually middle-aged white males), pimps and prostitutes, former mental hospital patients, Navy men on shore leave, and younger persons who work sporadically as waitresses, hotel staff, parking lot attendants, book store clerks. The hotel has a heterogeneous population, but is dominated by the presence of older retired persons.

After working several days as a desk clerk at the Ballentine, I was "briefed" by the manager on several of the tenants. The younger permanents, both men and women, either work in the area or are unemployed and on some type of public assistance. As the following account shows, hotel staff know a lot about residents:[*]

> Well Jimmie, the black guy, is about 32. He's not all there and talks a lot to himself. Winfred is in her late 20s and had a lot of hard luck. She drinks a lot and dances topless over on Broadway. It's okay to let her take guys up to her room. Susie is a little older, maybe 30. She has tried suicide several times and spent two and a half years in a mental hospital. Cally is a construction worker and lives with his girlfriend. Now Joe must be over 500 pounds; he eats too much; he often has food delivered to his room five or six times a day. Connie is about 19 and left her husband. She's trying to get a divorce; all the sailors she has up to her room create a problem. Earl is legally blind, but can see figures. He gets a disability check each

Fictitious names are used throughout

month, but can't manage it. Always pays the rent though. Smith is on welfare and lived with a girlfriend until she moved out.

Many of the middle-aged men and women (forty to sixty) have emotional problems and are under the care of mental health agencies (although I never saw a social worker visiting in the hotel).

> Ellen, well I don't know much about her except she's a CMH patient (community mental health). So is Bobby, Paul, Eric, and Joan. Bobby will come down every morning about 5 a.m., buy a Bubble-Up and then prance back and forth in the lobby drinking it and burping up a storm. Joan is in her 40s. She worked on the desk until I hired you. She gets depressed and is on a lot of medication. One night she lit a fire in the big ash tray by one of the sofas. I got real mad and told her we'd have none of that. She almost fainted in the lobby once.

Other residents adopt a "helping" role and aid those with drinking problems.

> Alice is the Florence Nightingale around here. She has power of attorney for Beatrice, who is senile and in her 80s. As long as Alice is here, Beatrice can stay. Alice's fiance got killed just before they were to get married. She never married and has worked as a waitress down here for years. Bernie, the alcoholic in room ___, is her boyfriend, but they haven't been speaking since his last binge. That whole group up on the fourth floor are alcoholics. Dave used to be a lawyer somewhere in the South and he knows the law. I can't evict 'em without a court order. Once you rent to them on a monthly basis, you can't just tell 'em to get out—they're permanent and it's the same as if they were living in an apartment. They drink together in their rooms and get all messed up. Alice goes and takes care of 'em. Stew is an alcoholic who's been sober for the past three years. He raised three girls single handed. His wife was an alcoholic and left him when the girls were all pretty young. He is hypertense and with his daughter having problems, well, I'm afraid he'll go to pieces. He's worked for me for two years.

Many of the older residents have lived in the downtown for many years. Several know one another, provide supportive services to each other, and view the hotel as their home.

Beatrice is senile and if it wasn't for Alice, she'd have to go. She is getting worse all the time. Insists that someone stole her T.V. and sometimes wanders out late at night. She hangs around with old Winston; they're about the same age. They always watch T.V. together; just about do everything together. They aren't married and met in the hotel. Winston is oppressed by women, just follows them around. Sergeant Finch drinks a lot and has a lot of trouble getting around. He is in his 70s and still fighting the war; swears he served in Vietnam. Both Harriet and Linda have lived here for years. Linda used to work as a waitress; Harriet ran a cheap hotel up the street until her husband died, then waitressed. Linda is over 70 and Harriet about 60-65. They think they own the place. I'm at war with them and some other permanents over painting the third and fourth floors. They fear the rent increases. I'd like to get rid of some permanents—I can make more money off transients.

Marty is in his 60s and has emphysema. He keeps oxygen in his room. Drinks way too much. He has three daughters, but they get tired of his calling them all hours of the day and night. He says that he is going to visit 'em, but goes to Detox instead (a detoxification center for alcoholics). Joanne must be in her late sixties. She has a daughter who comes to see her. They want to put her in a nursing home—she goes on drinking sprees—what a mess. I'm helping them to put her in a home. She's a fighter, likes her freedom. Allen has a bad attitude, talks a lot to himself and reads a lot. He gets around pretty good. Alfredo has been here for over 20 years. He is 86 and moved here after retirement and selling a restaurant back East. I don't think he'll be back from the hospital (he had a stroke and was in the hospital).

Orly is in his 80s; he is a professional gambler, always has been. He gets a call from his sister every Sunday evening, so if he's not in his room don't forget to check the T.V. room. He gets mad as hell if he misses that call. Now Sam lived in the same Italian neighborhood back East as Alfredo, but Sam keeps his distance. He gambles every day, all day; that's his life. Some don't like him, and Linda calls him a "snake."

James is the crippled guy on crutches. He's lived here for over ten years and has been severely crippled for the past seven. Harriet takes care of him—they used to be pretty close, but now Harriet sees Dennis, who lives on the second floor.

The population living in the Ballentine ranges from nineteen to over eighty years of age. Racially the tenants are predominantly white. However, there are five blacks, three Mexicans, and one Oriental living there as permanent residents. As a rule, the number of transients and minorities increases on the weekends.

Most older residents are not newcomers to the urban hotel environment. Several have lived in the same hotel for as long as twenty years, and the same room for over ten years. Some others have lived in the downtown for the larger part of their lives, but adopted a pattern of moving from one hotel to another. This pattern often results from interpersonal problems (in most cases related to alcohol) with other residents or the management. Over half of both males and females have never been married; the rest are widowed and divorced. No one is currently married and living with a spouse.

Work histories are in semiskilled and unskilled occupations. Some of the older women have worked in the downtown as bar maids, waitresses, or hotel clerks. Men's jobs range from lawyer to parking lot attendant. Some have made careers out of gambling, while others have just drifted from one manual job to the next in different areas across the country. Older residents' incomes are low, the primary sources being Social Security, V.A. pensions, and money picked up from sporadic part-time jobs.

Hotel residents have many health problems. Alcoholism, various disabilities and handicaps (vision and hearing loss, ambulatory difficulties), chronic conditions (stroke, emphysema, heart trouble), and emotional problems are prominent in the population. The sheer number of prosthetic devices (glasses, canes, walkers, wheel chairs, artificial limbs, hearing aids) visually portrays the level of physical disability. In general, the older residents (sixty-five and over) perceive themselves to be better off—they are the survivors. The most acute alcoholism and emotional symptomology is observed among those in their middle years.

In some low rent hotels, the concentration of physical

and emotional problems is greater than that found in the Ballentine. As mentioned earlier, chronic alcoholics and other problematic tenants not acceptable at the Ballentine often rent rooms at the adjacent General Lee Hotel. Thus, some hotels more than others become depositories for those with the severest disabilities and problems. The following statement was made by the manager at the General Lee Hotel and helps to illustrate the level of disability and impairment among some of the younger cohorts living there.

> We had an old man that died in there—it wasn't an old man, he was only 47 years old. I didn't know how young he was until he died. He lived up in one of the rooms and he had cirrhosis of the liver. He was nothing but skin and bones and tummy. He refused to go. I had the police there two days before, and they couldn't take him out of the room for any reason, health or otherwise unless you're unconscious, and he was still conscious. He wouldn't go. He was a veteran. I couldn't get him to go up there (to the Veterans Hospital) and they wouldn't send an ambulance. He had to go there. He wouldn't go. We used to have to go there in the morning about 9:00. I'd hear him, and I'd go help him out of bed, cause he couldn't get up again once he was lying flat on his back. Once he was up, he was okay, and he'd get to the bathroom or sit in his chair, but he never left his room, never left the hotel. He'd make it down to the bathroom. One morning we didn't hear him so we opened the door and checked, and he had died sometime during the night.

Demographically, older residents at the Ballentine are very similar to those living in other SRO hotels. A random sampling of seventy-five residents (reported on in detail in Chapter 10) in twelve hotels shows that the average age of older residents is sixty-two years. On the average, SRO hotels have approximately 10 percent older females living as permanent residents (as measured by six or more months of continuous residence in the hotel). The average level of education for older hotel residents is 9.5 years. Only 18 percent of the residents have worked in jobs at the clerical level or higher—most having been employed in skilled, semiskilled and unskilled occupations. Residents have an average monthly income of $301. Less than 20 percent of the residents are on welfare—predominantly those below retirement age who are unemployed. Those persons eligible for Social Security are on it—others are on civil service pension, military retirement, and disability.[3]

The residents of the Ballentine cite several advantages of living in a downtown hotel. At first, residents usually express the obvious advantage of low rent and convenience to shops, restaurants, and transportation. One older resident summed up the economic advantage of living in an SRO hotel and some of the choices they afford:

> I'm used to cheap hotels and rooming houses. You know, you grow up a certain way, and most of my life, I've been working by myself. I never made a lot of money where I can afford a nice apartment and pay like a hundred and thirty, and a hundred and forty a month rent. I'd rather do things with my money, like go to the race track, or eat good, like that, and pay less rent. If you're gonna pay less rent, you're gonna wind up in downtown hotels.

Closely associated with the economic benefits of hotel living is the privacy, freedom, and services they offer to residents.

The maintenance of independence and self-reliance is fostered in the SRO hotel. Within the confines of a minimal income, older persons pay their own way and are guaranteed the privacy of their own room, and the freedom to determine their own rhythms of eating, sleeping, coming and going.

The Ballentine makes minimal social demands on residents. Within the hotel environment, there are few expectations and responsibilities other than paying one's rent, and causing minimal "trouble." Hotels allow for a wider range of behavior than is permissible in other contexts (e.g., family households, apartments, middle-class hotels). For example, one man chose the Ballentine over family to maintain his freedom.

> Yeh, I tried living with my sister for a while, but it didn't work out. I like to get a few beers, maybe bring someone home I met. You know, well, she didn't go for that. I wasn't gonna give it up, so I moved down here.

While residents choose in most situations to handle problems themselves, the hotel staff is always available when problems become unmanageable. The care offered by the hotel staff is nonbinding and only semipersonal, thus minimizing feelings of dependency on the part of the older person. Additionally, hotel living frees them from telephone, gas, and electric bills, cooking and shopping, while at the same time providing basic housekeeping services and a desk clerk to contact at any time during the day or night. For the older residents, these features of the setting are essential for continued independent living.

A subtle aspect of hotel life is the benefit derived from being in close physical proximity to other people. In some cases, whether or not one interacts with others is secondary to simply feeling a part of something. For some, having access to other persons is a buffer to isolation—what is important is the potential for interaction. The environment provides the option for much or little social interaction. One man told me,

> I just sit here and watch the world go by. The best time is when the girls try and get, uh money from the sailors or when someone gets loaded . . . . A lot of people to watch here. From this chair I can see . . . I don't talk much to other tenants, just one or two. I've heard their stories, and I don't hear too well . . . . This is like my living room.

One desk clerk at the Ballentine commented, "Yeh, some of the old ones definitely view this place as home. They are financially able to live in better accommodations, but continue on here—they relate to the place somehow."

In this chapter I have given a generalized description of an SRO hotel, the Ballentine. It included a discussion of the physical layout of a medium sized hotel and an introduction to the people who live there. The next chapter will focus on the roles and functions of hotel staff as they interact with older tenants.

Notes

1   Of the twelve hotels sampled in the south of Broadway area, eight had
lobbies with chairs and sofas, four had T.V. viewing rooms, three had
restaurants located in the building, and three had elevators. They
ranged in size from 12 to 325 rooms.

2   Some hotels had more active maintenance programs; exteriors and
interiors were conscientiously kept up. For example, the Wells Fargo
Hotel had a reputation for its cleanliness and no-nonsense policies.
One desk clerk at the Wells Fargo stated: "We took no welfare
persons subsisting on welfare payments in the hotel—the basic reason
is that the hotel has been there since 1914, and had built a very good
reputation over the years. I can understand their policy, which hasn't
changed. The man running it today is running it just like the man
before. We had people from all over the world come to stay there—
cheap hotels, clean. It was in their books to come. It was rather
strange to me that it was still so, because Fourth Street has gotten to
be rather skid-rowish over the years. But still they don't take welfare,
because one of their basic policies is that they look the man up and
down."

3   Comparison of SRO hotels with middle class hotels is reported in R.J.
Erickson and J.K. Eckert, "The Elderly Poor in Downtown San Diego
Hotels," *The Gerontologist*, 17, no. 5 (October, 1977):440-46.

Street

C. Floor Plan

5
Caretakers and Exploiters: The Hotel Staff

Few early studies of hotel life addressed the interactions and interdependencies of hotel residents with the functionaires in the setting.[1] These studies started from the premise that SRO life is in "no way a social world." It is marked by the extremes of social disorganization, social isolation, impersonality, and anonymity. More recent studies have provided additional data characterizing hotel life as atomistic and fragmented.[2]

These later studies, however, have begun to recognize the importance of hotel staff, neighborhood shop owners, and various community services available in urban commercial zones in allowing for, and contributing to the individualistic character of hotel living. From the social transactions of these various people, the unique character or "social climate" of the SRO world emerges. In this chapter, the roles and positions of various "caretakers" will be examined. The term "caretaker" is adopted from Herbert Gans, *The Urban Villagers,* a study of an Italian community in Boston. As individuals and institutions offering care to members, the term "caretaker" can be applied broadly to anyone who offers services to people. It can be applied to hotel managers, desk clerks, maids, and waitresses. As stated by

Gans, "Caretaking is not an altruistic act, but a reciprocal relationship in which the caretaker gives his services in exchange for a material or nonmaterial return."[3]

Caretaking in the hotel environment provides formal and informal support to the older hotel residents. The primary caretakers for the older resident are those persons internal to the hotel setting—the hotel managers, desk clerks, and maids. These persons constitute the core support system which allows for the maintenance and character of hotel life.[5]

Caretakers and other SRO tenants are the two major groups with whom older residents must regularly interact. The first group includes the hotel staff, plus shop owners, and restaurant waitresses operating in the downtown. External to the hotel setting are the social/health system and other organizational caretakers. This group represents a culture (usually middle class) different and apart from the hotel culture. They enter the hotel culture on an intermittent basis to perform services and functions. This chapter will offer a descriptive analysis of the internal caretakers who affect the lives of the older hotel residents. The next chapter concerns those caretakers external to the hotel culture.

Caught in the Middle: The Hotel Manager

Hotel managers are the most important persons in the hotel culture. They provide it with form and structure. They carry out a wide range of acts, including the interpretation of hotel policies, dealing with the problems of staff and residents, and guiding the hotel in its dealings with the external world. In general, their training is scant—it was certainly no training that prepared them for their multifaceted job, and some are not adequately prepared by any means to do the job well. Shapiro has recognized that the managers of low rent hotels face considerable stress. They consider themselves businessmen, but often find themselves akin to directors of semi-institutions with untrained staff.[6]

The manager of the Ballentine Hotel, Shelly Spindler, has worked at the hotel for seventeen years. During the first twelve years, and under the past owner and manager, he worked as a desk clerk. Since the hotel's new owner took it over five years ago, Shelly has been the manager.[7] Shelly answers directly to the general manager of the hotel chain, Mr. Eldorado. The general manager sets the wage scales, keeps check on the overall financial health of the operation, and continually puts pressure on the individual hotel managers to keep expenses to a minimum and economize wherever possible.

Shelly has lived in the Ballentine since he first started to work there. When he became manager, he moved into a newly decorated one room "suite" on the second floor of the hotel. His quarters are easily distinguished from other rooms by the fancy door at the end of the hallway. Shelly began work in hotels in his late teens as a sheet sorter, worked his way up first to an elevator operator, then desk clerk. He is fond of reporting that before coming to the Ballentine "I worked in some of the best hotels and know this business."

Shelly's life revolves around the hotel. He is there twenty-four hours a day, commuting between his bedroom on the second floor and his small office behind the hotel's front desk. Only on Sundays does he leave the hotel to attend church and then have dinner with his mother and stepfather.

Shelly is restricted in some of the things he can do because he suffers from a handicap. For him managing the Ballentine is an ideal job, in part because it requires a minimum of physical activity and effort. As manager, Shelly uses his authority to get services from the desk clerks and maids—they are expected to run personal errands for him, work extra hours with little notice, and give emotional support. In addition to hotel staff Shelly has a pool of tenants on whom he relies for services—mainly running errands for food, cigars, or newspapers. In exchange for these services tenants are paid a small amount of money (usually $.50) and granted "favored status," which includes such benefits as a "line of credit" in lean times, extra towels, and general bending of the hotel rules and regulations in their direction.

The manager has power over the tenants and exercises

it. Tenants realize this and sometimes try to tap into this power. Only a few tenants—mostly the younger ones and those more functionally capable—provide direct services to the manager. Older tenants gain favor through a certain degree of deference and cordiality. Tenants who win Shelly's favor are granted privileges including some flexibility in rent payments and latitude in acceptable behavior. For example, one eighty-two-year-old man who had lived in the hotel for some years had become incontinent and on occasion soiled his bed linens and towels. Under most circumstances—and definitely with a new tenant—such behavior constitutes grounds for eviction. In this man's case, however, allowances were made. Another case involved a sixty-seven-year-old man who suffered from emphysema and required that oxygen be kept in his room. Because Shelly had known the man for years and liked him, he was allowed to stay in the hotel in spite of the fire hazard the oxygen presented. In another case, Shelly even resisted the demands of the general manager and refused to evict a tenant who, on several occasions, forgot to turn off his wash basin water, causing water damage to several rooms. He was able to work out an arrangement whereby the man paid for repairs to the damaged rooms.

The criteria for extending favors to certain tenants are never clearly articulated by the management. In some cases favored status rests on the sheer length of acquaintance. A few tenants lived in the hotel before Shelly started there as a desk clerk, and he is aware that the hotel is their only home. Paying on time, predictable and nontroublesome behavior (taking care of oneself, not drinking excessively) are important factors for gaining favored status.

The managements of most hotels show great awareness of their tenants; they know who has been living there for some time. At the Ballentine the manager feels ambivalence and even open hostility toward some tenants; toward others he expresses affection and friendship. Toward most of the older residents, he shows real benevolence, realizing the importance of the hotel to them. He usually knows which tenants are having health or drinking problems, what medications they take and what care they are under, and whom to call in an emergency. Some of this information is obtained directly from the resident, some from the maids, some from the gossip of other tenants. Most of the older residents give Shelly the name of a person to contact should they become severely ill or die suddenly.

The gulf between the manager and his charges varies considerably. In some larger hotels, where the management is better trained, the social distance from the tenants is more pronounced—they view themselves as business executives and expect their staff to deal directly with the residents. At the Ballentine, the manager is concerned with day-to-day operations and less with the financial aspects of the hotel business. His staff is poorly trained and overworked. Thus, he comes in contact with tenants on a regular basis. Many residents criticize Shelly's behavior as idiosyncratic and question his intellectual capacity to run the hotel. Those that remember him as "just a desk clerk" feel he was promoted because "they could get him cheap; if they threw him out, he'd be on a bread line."

The majority of verbal transactions between tenants and management involve relatively impersonal and superficial statements about the weather, sports, or other items reported in the paper or heard on television. Personal matters involving family or feelings, if discussed, are done so in a joking manner.

Few older residents confront Shelly directly with complaints about the hotel or how it is run. However, residents do share their negative feelings with other tenants and hotel employees. Some tenants would approach me as desk clerk and converse about the manager's actions (or lack of action). They would frequently reveal their dislike for Shelly, other clerks, and residents. Most of the permanent residents are critical of the manager. However, on the basis of some older residents' cordial and gregarious interactions with Shelly, it would be difficult to assess their true feelings toward him. Surprisingly, Shelly seemed unaware of the contempt many residents feel toward him. In fact, when I first started working at the Ballentine, Shelly was in the habit of saying, "Kevin, we're just one big happy family here; a home away from home you might say." If there was any irony, it did not show.

Shelly's unpredictable behavior carried over to dealings with the hotel employees. Unpredictable mood swings, rapid changes in hotel operating procedures and regulations created problems for the clerks, especially those who felt particularly dependent on the job.

Some of the hotel's employees have chronic employment problems related to alcoholism or some disability (mental or physical). Because they are highly unlikely to find jobs in other contexts, they tolerate a considerable amount of authoritarian treatment from the manager. The level of dependence some employees exhibit allows Shelly to manipulate them for his own purposes. The level of discontentment is chronically high among employees, yet few confront Shelly with their complaints. Employees recognize that their job prospects are dim; they placate the manager and hope to stay in his favor.

Hotels vary in the degree of permissive behavior they allow. Hotels that enforce few rules and regulations tend to be the most open. Such hotels accept residents with the most severe cases of alcoholism, drug addiction, mental and physical disability. They also tend to have the largest percentage of younger adults and minorities. Hotels that enforce strict rules and regulations ipso facto have the least behavioral nonconformity and least illicit activity. The Ballentine falls midway in the permissiveness-restraint continuum, but it fluctuates over time. According to most older tenants, the hotel is becoming too permissive about rules and allowable tenants (older tenants are afraid that the number of blacks and other minorities will increase).

Actually, the enforcement of hotel rules fluctuates on an ad hoc basis. Shelly's enforcement of the rules depends on personal moods, incidents, and pressures from the general manager. For example, a new night clerk at the Ballentine was directed by Shelly to call the police for any difficulties she might encounter while working the shift. Shelly made it clear that he did not wish to be disturbed during the night. The past clerk had been extremely lenient in allowing prostitutes and alcoholics into the hotel during the night. The new clerk attempted to stop the pattern—thus, she encountered several arguments and altercations with prostitutes and their clients. Following the manager's orders, she called the police for assistance. The police felt that they were being called too frequently for matters that were not serious, so they notified the general manager and questioned him about the kind of hotel he was running. The result was a new directive from the general manager—do not call the police except in the most serious circumstances. If assistance was needed, he said the clerk should call Shelly and let him handle the matter. Clerks soon learn that Shelly can do little to assist them in such matters. Instead of struggling to follow the rules, clerks simply become more permissive and blase in their efforts to enforce regulations. They become socialized to their jobs and learn to cooperate and not to cause trouble.

Older tenants are sensitive to the various types of persons and activities allowed in the hotel. From their perspective, the hotel is becoming a less desirable place to live—there is (they say) more prostitution, more alcoholism, and more minorities. They blame such changes on the manager and his incompetence.

From Shelly's perspective, he is "caught in the middle." He needs the job and believes that there are not many job opportunities elsewhere. While lamenting the changes in the hotel, he has no alternative but to rent rooms to those who present themselves. In order to keep the vacancy rate low and the general manager happy, he rents rooms to almost anyone, barring only the most disturbed and disoriented customers.

Shelly briefs clerks on how to "size up customers." In sizing up a customer, several obvious factors are taken into consideration. Age, hair style, clothing, and race are immediate factors of importance. For example, if the customer is young with shorter hair and casually dressed, he is probably in the military and in the downtown for some excitement and relaxation. He is charged the full room rate. Such men are preferred transient clients, since they have money, and attract to the hotel other customers following and feeding off them, i.e., prostitutes, homosexuals, and con men. Younger black men are usually pimps who rent rooms for themselves and their "wives."[8] They are also charged full price, and sometimes an extra fee for each individual taken up to their room (clerks vary in charging the additional fee). Minority families, especially Mexican families who cannot speak English, are offered rooms at slightly reduced rates. Older persons, poorly dressed and who balk at the room rates, are offered slightly reduced rates rather than lose their business to another hotel. Rate reductions are not given out of concern for the customer, but as a means of renting rooms. Reducing room rates is more common during the slower winter months and on weekdays throughout the year. Downtown hotels are full on weekends all year and every day during the summer months.

Managers vary in their efforts to control and exert power over tenants. These efforts are related to several factors. Some managers that overcontrol are insecure in their positions in the management hierarchy—through maintenance of control and order, they attempt to stabilize their positions. Other managers are high on helping (and exploiting) older tenants and view tight control as beneficial to them. For example, some control whom the residents see and under what conditions. This practice is viewed by some managers as "protecting the residents" from persons who would otherwise take advantage of them.

In an effort to increase his control, Shelly instituted a procedure of having all guests "sign up" before visiting residents. In this way, a record was kept of who from outside the hotel was visiting what room. If visitors remained upstairs past 10:00 p.m., they were called by the desk clerk and asked to leave or pay a $3.00 overnight charge. In Shelly's words, "this procedure protects the guests; we know who is up there, how long, and how many. If we have trouble, we know what we're up against." This policy was adopted after an attempted rape in one of the rooms.

In most cases, overt efforts to control residents revolve around those with drinking problems. During the time I worked at the Ballentine, a group of middle-aged men with drinking problems were living there. Shelly was aware that two of these men were alcoholics. They had previously lived in the hotel, but had moved out for various reasons. Shelly allowed them back into the hotel on the belief that they were "on the wagon" and had "reformed." Approximately three weeks after they moved back into the hotel one of the men began to drink heavily. The spree lasted for over thirty days. When the first man began to sober up, two others started a spree. The total number of men involved in the drinking group grew to four and all lived in rooms on the same floor. Over a period of two months, their behavior began to create problems. They would gather in one room, talk loudly, fall in the hallway and bathrooms, and on a few occasions verbally abuse the older tenants. In Shelly's words, "They mess up the bathrooms and ruin my rooms." As the number of complaints mounted, Shelly began a process of trying to get them out of the hotel. In past instances, Shelly had refused the room rent and locked the troublesome tenant out. In this instance, one of the drinking group had operated a hotel and knew that persons who rented rooms on a monthly basis could not legally be "locked out" of a room. They had to be served eviction notices or be caught drunk in a public place with liquor in their possession.

Shelly had never been confronted with this kind of challenge to his power. What followed was an involved process of trying to catch each of the drinking group in a drunken state outside of their rooms. Over several weeks, and with the cooperation of desk clerks and maids, Shelly was able to "set up" each drunken tenant so that the police could legally arrest them for public drunkenness. After a long and involved process, the management was able to break up the drinking group.

Soon after the last one of the group was gone, Shelly changed hotel policy so that rooms were rented to new tenants on a daily or weekly basis, but not by the month. Customers desiring monthly rates had to first rent on a weekly basis (usually for one month) so that Shelly could personally "size them up."

There are several ways in which the management can censure troublesome tenants. The most extreme measure involves the "plugging" of a room. In hotel terms, this means that half a key is inserted into the door lock of a room, thus blocking the resident's key from fitting the lock. The management has the other half of the key that will open the door. Residents view plugging as a serious action, since it not only deprives them of their only private space but often separates them from their possessions. During my tenure at the Ballentine, I witnessed only two incidences of plugging as a means of eviction. In both cases, the men were problem drinkers overdue on their rent payments. Locking out tenants literally "puts them on the street." With their possessions locked away and money resources depleted, they are left in a helpless position.

In one case, a man in his late sixties was locked out when his room was "plugged." He had no much and the maids say he dirties his sheets." After giving him several warnings either to remain in the hotel, he had the maid put his possessions in a plastic rubbish bag and locked them away in the storeroom. When the man returned, he had no room, nor would Shelly hand over his belongings. The man sat in the lobby for over twenty-four hours arguing, threatening, and sleeping. Shelly's patience finally ran short; he gave the man his possessions and told him to get out of the hotel. Shelly then called the other hotels in the chain and warned them not to rent to the man.

To the manager's dismay, some tenants do challenge his authority and power. One young black tenant asked the management not to allow maids to enter his room. A maid violated his order, and he later claimed that some of his possessions had been stolen. He pressed charges against hoth Shelly and the maid and won a hundred dollars in damages. Instances such as this test the management's authority and cuase them to become increasingly defensive and uncertain in their positions. Again, in this instance, Shelly complained about being caught in the middle—this time between the tenants and the law. While the balance of power between tenants and the management was not equal at the Ballentine, things were changing more in favor of the tenants.

Although the use of physical force by the management is infrequent, it does occur. In the case of one drunken tenant, a trap was set in which the management falsely told the tenant that someone was in the lobby to see him. When the drunken tenant came to the lobby, a maid quickly "plugged" his door lock. When the tenant realized that he had been tricked, he tried to get back to his room and fell while climbing the stairs. The manager and the maid physically abused the tenant and planted a bottle of wine on him, then called the police. The tenant was charged with public drunkenness.

As mentioned above, Shelly makes distinctions among the types of tenants in the hotel. The transients tend to be younger than the permanent residents and (in the management's words) "cause more trouble." The manager is less willing to tolerate problematic behavior from the transients and makes a greater effort to control their behavior. For example, the ruling that persons must "sign in" to the hotel is directed at controlling the number of visitors to transient rooms. The manager is also more likely to label the transient group as "deviant" or somehow tainted. Failure to pay rent on time, too many visitors, and other "troublesome" behavior meet with little sympathy. As was discussed earlier, permanent residents are treated with greater tolerance. In general, they are not stereotyped as "nuts," "mentals," or "losers," but simply as "old" and "poor."

The greater degree of tolerance shown to permanent tenatns is not based solely on sympathy for the factors of age and poverty. Permanent tenants are crucial to the hotel economy—they are the "bread and butter" of the operation. The manager depends on a certain percentage of permanent tenants to provide a stable source of operating capital. From Shelly's viewpoint,

> The permanents pay the overhead—they pay the bills and we can rely on them since they aren't gonna be leaving. Transients are the profit, we can make more off of them, but they create the trouble. You gotta have a percentage of clients that you can rely on.

The management attempts to create a manageable ratio of permanents to transient guests.

> You can't get too many permanents or too many transients. When we were up to around 80 percent permanents, that was just too many—we weren't making enough money. Now we're about 70 percent, and I want to get it lower, maybe 50 percent. When they die or go to a home, or move on, I'll change that room into a transient room. I can make more off the transients in one weekend than I can off the permanents in a month. Transients cost more though: they ruin the rooms, cause trouble, and they're not reliable, but if we get more, we make more money.

It is highly unlikely that the older permanent tenant will move away from the hotel. The determinants of low rent, more freedom than they could enjoy elsewhere, minimal social demands and responsibilities, a hotel staff available for emergency assistance, and a strong desire for privacy and independence lock them into the hotel. From their perspective, the hotel "fits" their personal values, economic limitations, and social needs producing an outcome that they evaluate as tolerably fair. Older residents who leave the hotel to visit relatives, change hotels, go to a hospital or nursing home, often return to the Ballentine. Dissatisfaction with family living, the hospital, or nursing home make the hotel the preferred environment.

Older residents present the manager with difficulties quite distinct from those presented by other tenants. In Shelly's words,

> The older ones get sick now and then, some forget, some leave water running, or burn something on those hot plates. Some even get to the point where they can't manage their money or take care of themselves. That's when you gotta step in and get a social worker to try and get 'em into a home. You

know, I never see one's family come and take 'em. But the families sometimes work with me in getting them into a home. Sometimes I do it myself—I do the signing and have them committed. They never want to go, but it's for their own good.

Around the Clock: Hotel Desk Clerks

Hotel desk clerks provide formal and informal service to hotel residents. They also are responsible for the hour by hour operations of the hotel. At the Ballentine there are four desk clerks, each responsible for his or her own shift. There is one person who regularly works the day shift (8:00 a.m. - 4:00 p.m.), swing shift (4:00 p.m. -12:00 p.m.), "graveyard" shift (12:00 p.m. - 8:00 a.m.) and "relief" shift (Monday and Tuesdays, 12:00 p.m. - 8:00 a.m., Wednesday and Thursday, 4:00 p.m. - 12:00 p.m., Sunday 8:00 a.m. - 4:00 p.m.). Day duty is the preferred shift, and the clerk with the most seniority works "up" to that position. Swing shift is less preferred, yet more popular than either "graveyard" or "relief." The manager has continual difficulty in finding steady employees for both of these shifts.

A frequent pattern in the Ballentine and other SRO hotels is for clerks to be recruited from the pool of unemployed middle aged tenants. For some clerks, the job is perceived as an opportunity to "learn the hotel business." The reasoning goes that working behind the desk will open opportunities and experiences for advancement in the same hotel or elsewhere. In most cases, this idea is frustrated through growing dissatisfaction with low wages or personal problems.

The major problems that face desk clerks center on controlling, helping, and minimizing personal involvement with the tenants. The clerks are central in the social and communication networks of the hotel. They are in direct contact with residents, they handle their mail, control their visitors, place and receive their telephone calls, and take personal messages. In many cases when residents have a need or a problem, the desk clerk is the first person they contact. A continuing problem for the clerk is how to be helpful without getting too involved in the lives of the residents. Many persons ask for favors; the clerk is continually trying to decide who he can trust. With time, clerks become embittered and selective about tenants' requests.

Sammy Hinkle is the senior clerk at the Ballentine. He has worked in the hotel for two years and has been a permanent resident there for over three years. He is fifty-six years old. His story is typical of other persons working and living in downtown hotels. The account of his job and life gives insight into the attitudes of clerks toward residents and the management as well as the life trajectory into hotel life.

> I'm fifty-six years old, was born in a midwest city and lived there until I was eleven. Up until that time, I lived with my mother, stepfather, stepbrother, and sister. My mother and real father got divorced when I was three years old. I never even thought of my stepbrother or sister that way—we got along real well. Even with my stepfather, I had a better relationship than with my father. From eleven to sixteen, I lived on and off with my real father and his new wife. There were some problems, so I lived with various relatives. I lived with aunts, uncles, maternal grandmother. I lived with so many people I can't remember them all. I never had any constancy during that time. I liked living with my uncle on his farm the best. I did that in the summers. It was quite an experience. I thought I was being abused, but with time, I've come to think it was beneficial to me.
>
> I felt my father didn't have any interest in me as a person. As it turned out, he didn't. I had a normal relationship with my mother, and as I grew older, it got better with my stepfather. My mother died just last month. She was disabled in later years and couldn't move around too well. Over the past year or so I've travelled to Los Angeles at least once every two months to see her.
>
> As a youngster, I always worked. At seventeen I had a big hassle with my mother and stepfather so I moved out and worked at Wrigley Field. I spent the summer down there.
>
> When I turned eighteen, I entered the service. That was a good experience. I was in Europe but saw little action. I guess I scored high in the tests because they gave me desk work. I climbed up the ranks and made Sergeant. It was great to have some authority. I'm small, and I've always been a little self-

conscious of that. I enjoyed leading around all those giants—
kind of ironic, I thought. Anyway, the military was pretty
good until I got sick. I came down with a rare kind of heart
condition so had to leave Europe and come back to the States.
I met my first wife when I returned. We dated for a short
time, got married, and then started having children. We had
three daughters in five years.

Things weren't too bad during those days. We lived in L.A.
and bought a little house. I was making a reasonable salary
working as an insurance salesman. Well, after the third child,
things went haywire. My wife was drinking—she became an
alcoholic. One day she left home and, this is hard to believe, I
never heard from her again. The police tried to locate her,
but no luck. She was *gone*. It took me a couple of years to get
over that, and I still don't understand how any woman could
take off and abandon her children.

After she left, I got a housekeeper and went about raising
three daughters. I remarried in my early thirties, but that
lasted only two years. After the divorce, I gave up on
marriage. I dated and got out on the town but started to drink
heavily. I got transferred to San Diego with the insurance
company and was under too much pressure—kids, work,
everything. The drinking got worse. I'd go off and not come
home. I'd end up in a hotel or on the street—a real mess. I lost
my job with the insurance company. By the way, the girls
were all older, so it wasn't like I'd abandoned them. They
were having their problems too. One turned out to be a
delinquent and still is at thirty-three.

With the job loss, everything else went—the house, then the
family broke up. I flopped around from hotel to hotel. I was
continually being arrested for public drunkenness. Sometimes
they'd throw me in jail and other times they'd let me off. I
tried sobering up a few times. My brother even offered me a
job and set me up in a travel business. I went up to L.A. and
worked at it but then started drinking, and the business failed.
He gave me a break, but I fucked it up. I also ran a flop house
in town for about two years.

The pattern got worse until I came up before a judge here in
town who'd seen me once too many times. He said that a man
with my background shouldn't live as I do and that he never
wanted to see me again in his court. He sent me to a work
farm for one year where I received psychiatric care and had

time to think. It had an influence on me. I got out just about three years ago.

When I got out, I moved into the Ballentine. I had a small V.A. disability so couldn't afford anyplace else. After about nine months, Shelly offered me a job. Actually, the general manager hired me. Shelly was uptight about his job since he knows I could run this place more competently than he. I needed a job so grabbed the clerk job. I figured I'd eventually work up to managing one of the other hotels in the chain.

It's been convenient living and working here, but it's depressing. Shelly is tyrannical with his power. You know how he calls down to the desk and expects us to wait on him bringing him coffee and cookies. I say let the bastard do it himself. But if you don't go along, he'll make it tough, so I go along with it and keep quiet. What really makes it difficult is that he changes his mind at the drop of a hat. One day he wants it this way, next day that way. A hopeless way to run a hotel.

The place has really gone downhill the past few years. Even when I came here, I thought it was a nicer place. The general manager is "milking" it. Christ, everybody uses everybody for all they're worth these days. I suppose they will continue to get what they can from the hotel until the area is redeveloped, then they'll make it into a parking lot or something.

I like some of the people here, mostly the older ones though. You get to know them with time. You start being closer. If someone treats me more generously, then you try to accommodate them. You give what you can simply because they have treated you like a decent human being. If they give you a hard time, then you don't bother with 'em. With time, you get hard. People come in and treat you a certain way, so you get cautious. I've had people come in and make demands. They want this and that—don't have manners. I try to accommodate people but a lot less now than at first. You get tougher with time.

You get to know about some of the older ones. About seven have been in the hotel for over ten years. They are fixtures and definitely view the hotel as home.

What's surprising is that they (the permanents) really don't have groups even though they've lived here for five or so years. You'd think they would get together over common interests like betting on the horses or playing cards. In the hotel, they just don't associate that much with one another. They do, but it's pretty much in passing. It's a lobby type of thing. Now there are a few instances. Like Linda and Harriet have known each other for years. They help each other and some of the older men as well. When one of the permanents gets sick, people do make an effort to help. If somebody goes to the hospital, everybody is calling, they wanna know where they are and how they are doing. Recently, when Mr. Hayes got sick, everybody was calling. Some residents were going down to his room taking care of him. I had no idea they knew him that well or were interested, so they are taking care of him as if he was their own brother. They leave notes on the desk for them to be called if anything happens. When somebody is sick, you have a whole chain of rooms you gotta call. Now, when somebody is in the hospital, they call and wanna talk to three or four of their friends. These are the things I don't even see in the lobby, but when these people get sick and someone is helping them out, it's almost as if they'd been together for a lifetime. Sickness is very important for the elderly, they all come to the front when someone is sick.

About four of them go out to dinner on Sundays on a regular basis. I've been invited but never went. See, I just don't trust Harriet. She's always trying to find out about me. They see me with a clean shirt and tie and think I have money. There is the group that is always in the T.V. room. Same three or four day after day.

Another group that come to mind was three people—Marilyn and two men. They were all released from State hospitals when Reagan closed 'em down a few years back. For about seven or eight months they did everything together. They were constantly together until one of the men moved to the East Coast. They were on the street together, the lobby, coffee together, lunch at a certain time. It never deviated. Marilyn is still here. She even worked at the desk for a time, but it got to be too much. She's better with no pressure.

Come to think of it we've had quite a few ex-mental hospital patients in the hotel. Some do pretty well, then others just aren't ready. We have several in here now. Some never come out of their room, and when they do, they never talk to you. There is one woman who lived here for months. I've never said more than two words to her. She never talks to anyone. Ted is improving, he was the same way at first, but now talks more.

We get all kinds in the hotel—young and old. You name it, and we get it. Over half are retired and on Social Security or some kind of pension. Some others live here for three or four months—maybe on welfare or just broke up with their wives or girlfriends. We have people with all sorts of problems. Drinking seems to be the big one though. We've had drinking groups establish where they are door to door [adjacent rooms]. Some will go on drinking sprees for thirty to sixty days, falling down drunk in their rooms and in the hallways. I might mention that within the law, it's very hard to get rid of those people. I had a police officer actually catch one in the hallway with a bottle of wine (which is public as opposed to room which is private) and wouldn't do anything. A policeman can't take them out of their room. We had one individual who was drunk and causing trouble. The management got the police and the guy jumped in bed with his clothes on. He didn't even lock his door and said, "You can't take me." He was bombed but had enough sense to do that. The officer said, "He's right, a few years ago I could take him by the neck and drag him out, but I can't do it now."

The maids pretty much know what's going on with people. They get into the rooms and see the tenants so have an idea if they're drinking or not eating or doing too well. We've had a couple of old ones who've been sick. You take Alfredo. Well, at 86 he shouldn't even be here. The maids and Linda try to help him out. I hate to see him out on the street. He could drop dead any minute. I think he should be in some controlled situation where people could help him. He doesn't want that though. He wants to be in the hotel. Actually, it works a hardship on all of us in the hotel. It's an annoyance. He has to take his medicines so he comes to me or a maid and wants us to read the label. He can't communicate in English anymore, only a little Italian, and even that is poor since his stroke. Well, he takes the wrong medicine—like pills for his heart instead of vitamins. He's done that on several occasions. He can't read the labels, gets confused, takes the wrong stuff, then sits in the lobby like a zombie. But he always comes back to the hotel because Linda and Harry speak Italian and they can understand him. Some others speak Italian down here. They help him, especially Linda. It's been his home for twenty-one years.

We have a high turnover of maids. The good ones are hard to keep at these wages. We get some that are losers. We have inventory losses, and the service is not that good. When a maid takes time and cleans a room, the management says that they spend too much time. Some maids ingratiate themselves with the tenants. They'll borrow money and then quit. Some come in there and make their real money through prostitution. We had complaints that one left "rubbers" under the pillows of newly made beds. We have one maid right now who is making a fuss over one of the elderly men. She gives him all this attention, and as a result, gets him to pay her room rent. In another case, I saw a maid being solicitous to an old man and afterwards walking away stuffing five twenties into her pocket. It's a con game, and some older tenants are victimized. It's not the rule, but I know of two cases. We get some bad ones, but the management hires the ones that he can get something from.

It's a good thing we have maids to check the rooms since some, mostly old ones, die in their rooms. On weekends the maids make up the beds in only the transient rooms, so we've had cases where a tenant will die on Friday and not be found till Monday. That happened with Rob Baxter. I knew him at the Cavalier Hotel. He had a room across from me. He had a drinking problem and had taken counseling and rehabilitation but couldn't kick it. When his sister died, she left him some money. That was just before moving here. His two daughters had given up on him—he made a pest of himself. He'd call them at all hours; especially when he had been drinking. Well, he died alone in his room. He'd been drinking heavily. It was a heart attack combined with an overdose of alcohol and medication. Sylvia, the maid, hadn't seen him for several days, so she and Shelly went up to the room and knocked on the door. They got no answer so had the police come and kick the door down. They found him on the floor. He'd been dead for three days.

That particular incident upset several of the old timers. Just the idea that they could lay dead in a room for several days. Since then, Shelly has the maids knock on all the doors to check up on people. We've had a few younger ones almost die from drug overdoses. That's really sad.

In general, there is not too much control in the hotel. Shelly is interested in making a buck, so we rent rooms when we can. What it comes down to is each individual clerk. I watch who I rent to, and that way I know who is in the rooms. What burns me up is that some clerks are irresponsible. They'll rent to anyone and fill up the rooms with people who'll cause us trouble. Then you end up getting calls about all the noise in this room or that room. Sometimes the talking gets too loud, so no one can sleep. That's when you end up running around keeping a lid on. I'm pretty small so I ask myself why I go on the line for $2.00 an hour.

Last year we had one clerk in here who was on night shift and had a real operation. This guy would allow prostitutes in here for a cut rate, never record the room as rented, and pocket the money. He'd allow the same prostitute to use the same room for half a dozen jobs. This guy wouldn't even change the sheets. Shelly finally fired him. I'm not sure why, I don't think he knew about the little business.

Although we do have some disruptive behavior in the hotel, it's mostly caused by the transients. The older people are decent people. I don't mean they don't have little problems, you know. Some go off and have their little drink. By and large, we are fortunate considering the area the hotel is in.

We do have security problems. All hotels have this problem, so I don't think we're an exception. It's hard to keep an eye on everything, especially when you're forced to leave the desk. That's a bad situation and shows the money making orientation of the business. I've heard that people have trouble when they invite someone to their room. You know, they get their checks, go out and have a drink, then invite someone back to their rooms. Some get mugged. You just can't go out and trust someone right off—some are just not that selective.

Then again, some go out and spend their money with little consideration, so when they sober up they'll say that someone ripped them off. I know all about that. They want sympathy and think maybe you'll loan them some money. Some use the rip-off thing as an excuse for not being responsible with their money. We get people complaining about room robberies. I don't think it's fact. I do believe it's mostly a hard luck story to get you to loan them a buck. I do that for some people. I've lost a few dollars, but most are good by their word.

Fires are a chronic problem here. Between you and me, I think someone has it out for us—five fires in not even four months. We've been lucky that they've all been confined to rooms, but one day maybe not. So far, no one has been injured, and I just keep my fingers crossed. The last one caused about $10,000 in smoke and water damage. What bothers me is that they leave the rooms go and don't repair them. We have three rooms out of order now, so we lose money. They are too cheap to repair the rooms, yet could cover the cost of repair with two weeks rent. It makes no sense to me.

Some old ones do better than others. Well it depends on their problems of course. Overall, I'd say they'd rather be here than in a home or living with relatives. Some leave the hotel and visit family, but they always come back and seem happy about returning. They get freedom and don't have people telling them what to do every minute. There is a lot of self-reliance among them considering their problems. Take Harvey. At eighty-three he has a pacemaker. He's furiously independent. I think he has always had a good self-image and nothing takes that away. He never complains—but most of them never complain about their lives.

Some don't do well, so we have to take action. Joanne, for example, moved in here from an apartment. She was afraid— no security, no one to call on in emergencies. She and her daughter checked around and put her in here. At first, it seemed to work, but she started hitting the bottle hard. She'd go for a week and finally become such a mess that we'd call her daughter who'd come down and take her for a few days. It got worse, and we finally decided she should go. Shelly and her daughter worked to get her into a home, but she didn't want to go. Finally, she locked herself in her room and wouldn't let anyone in. They got the police who had to help in getting her out. It was very sad. They put her in a home. They hate that more than anything—it's the end, and they resist it.

As for me, I want to get out of the downtown. I need to get away from the area and always go somewhere on my days off. Working here is just a job—it's the poor pay, the hassles, just not going anywhere. I've solved my drinking problem, so might go into business with my brother. He's offered to try again. Being here and seeing the drunks has helped me to know I don't want that again.

The demands placed on a desk clerk vary with the particular shift they are working. Clerks working the day shift have multiple duties and strains. They must deal with Shelly, the maids, the residents, and new customers. Some strains are lessened when the maids give assistance with the operation of the elevator or Shelly covers at the desk. The most important task for the day clerk is to make sure that transients either check out of their rooms or pay for another day. It is the clerk's responsibility to get them out of the room and get the key back.

There is little chance for boredom during the day shift and time goes quickly: maids up and down elevator; Shelly on the phone or in the lobby talking with someone; tenants coming and going; checking their mail, or sitting in the lobby.

The major responsibility of the person working "swing" shift is to rent rooms. Most new customers arrive in the late afternoon, thus, especially on weekends, the clerk is extremely busy checking in new people.

Peak activity at the desk usually coincides with residents coming and going for their afternoon meal. Operating the elevator, telephone switchboard, and checking in customers often becomes a mad rush from one thing to the next. After 8:00 p.m. or 9:00 p.m., activities settle down. The "regulars" are usually in place in the lobby and T.V. room. Transients are in and out of the hotel hustling or being hustled. The clerk working this shift has the greatest opportunity to converse with residents. There are usually one or two persons who hang around the desk and "keep you company."

The type of transient clientele checked into the hotel during the swing shift determines the amount and kind of troubles encountered on the night shift. On weekends a large percentage of military and prostitutes can make the night shift quite busy. In general, however, the specific duties needing attention can be completed in less than one hour. The tasks include updating records on occupancy rate, tenant head counts, updating each tenant's bill, filling out the cash sheet of the day's profits. The night shift allows time for reading or taking cat naps. However, most trouble occurs on this shift. Disruptive tenants elicit the most complaints at night, robberies and fires occur, and people get sick.

Barring trouble, the night shift allows for a clerk's involvement in schemes to make extra money. Such a scheme was reported in Sammy Hinkle's account.

The person working the night shift becomes acutely aware of individuals having problems. Persons not able to sleep sit the night in the lobby. Sometimes they talk, other times just sit quietly. I experienced one instance where an older permanent with a number of health problems began sleeping regularly in the lobby. He confided that he could not sleep when alone in his room. In the lobby he was with someone and felt more secure.

Some tenants select various clerks as favorites. For example, several older tenants told me that they wished I was the steady "swing" shift clerk. Their reason was my willingness to turn on the heat (during the winter months) at their request. The policy was not to turn on the heat until 10:00 p.m. I turned it on when people said they were cold. In exchange for my cooperativeness, I would receive small favors such as an occasional ice cream cone or piece of cake. One older tenant who I was particularly fond of gave me a pipe, stating, "You're a good boy and anyway, I got more pipes than I need. Just rinse it out with some whiskey." This was given in return for a specific favor of retrieving some keys from behind a dresser too heavy for him to move.

All in a Day's Work: Maids

The job of a hotel maid is a low paying extension of housework. As with clerks, maids are not unionized and are often subjected to degrading treatment, poor working conditions, arbitrary layoffs, and covert intimidation.

In its broadest outline, the job entails keeping rooms clean and furnished with linens and bathroom supplies. In the Ballentine, a single maid is frequently responsible for cleaning the entire hotel. In a recent article, Ryan[9] reports that in better hotels chambermaids are responsible for twelve and sixteen rooms and as many as twenty-two rooms in cheaper hotels. At the Ballentine, a maid has at the minimum thirty-five rooms to look after. Her duties also include the cleaning of bathrooms, hallways, and the lobby. The maid is responsible for keeping her cart stocked with linens and cleaning supplies, for carrying out trash, soiled linens, and for sorting linens. She must make periodic runs to replenish her linen stock. Other demands on her time are taken by interactions with tenants. In an average day, a maid may clean and change the linen in up to twenty rooms and make the beds in an additional ten to fifteen.

Most of the maids at the Ballentine are either black or Mexican-American. They frequently complain about their poor health and the continual bending, lifting, and pushing. On many occasions, I would be asked to assist in pushing a linen cart in and out of the elevator. I was at least forty pounds heavier than any one of the maids and found the task backbreaking.

A maid's work pattern is frequently thrown off through encounters with residents and the manager. Residents checking out of rooms late or not wishing to be disturbed delay the work pattern and cause a maid to work late into the afternoon. Desk clerks often rent rooms and then push maids to prepare them hurriedly for the new occupants. Additional pressures come from the manager who expects maids to give him extra attention, and in some instances sexual favors. Some maids succumb to the pressures at risk of losing their job. The pay is low, demands great, but jobs are difficult to come by and the pool of unskilled labor is large. As a group, maids are unskilled and poorly educated. They cannot qualify for better jobs nor can they afford the time or expense of additional training.

Maids desiring to do a good job are hounded by the management not to take too much time. Quantity, not quality, is the procedural dictum. Their work situation is less stable and viewed as inferior to the desk clerk. They are not guaranteed an eight hour day, and frequently get less time in the winter seasons and on weekdays. Unlike waitresses and cab drivers, maids receive little or no money from tips.

At the Ballentine, maids answer directly to the manager or desk clerk on duty. Some maids lived in the hotel and were subject to around-the-clock calls from the manager. In one case, the manager called a "live in" maid after work hours and ordered that linens be changed in several rooms. The maid refused to work after hours and was fired immediately, without recourse. Maids are also abused by residents (drunk and sober) who complain about rooms, demand services, or sexual favors.

In his book *Tally's Corner*, Elliot Liebow points out that among the advantages of working in hotels, restaurants, office and apartment buildings are the opportunities afforded for stealing on the job.[10] Inventory loss is a chronic problem in the Ballentine. Losses are high on such items as cleaning and bathroom supplies, bed linens, towels, and bedspreads. Such losses are attributed to the housekeeping staff. Liebow points out that stealing on the job is a two-edged sword. He states that,

> Apart from increasing the costs of the goods or services to the general public, a less obvious result is that the practice usually acts as a depressant on the employee's own wage level. Owners of small retail establishments and other employers frequently anticipate employee stealing and adjust the wage rate accordingly.[11]

The assumption that employees will steal the unpaid value of their labor penalizes those who do not steal. Additionally, the "wage-theft system" builds mutual distrust into the relationship between the employee and employer, creating a no-win situation for everyone.

Maids have several other strategies for supplementing their wages. The most common strategy is to gain "favor" with the manager and become his "special girl." This strategy can elevate a maid to a higher status than other maids as well as give her preference on days off, additional hours, and less work. Another tactic is to cultivate several tenants and become personally involved with them. For some this practice can double or triple their weekly salary. I observed one situation in which a maid fussed over an older tenant having a drinking problem. She became his "girlfriend," bought his liquor, and took care of him in exchange for his paying her room rent. In this situation, other residents gossiped and disapproved of the maid's conduct. A concerned resident told me, "Carmen is just using Smith. She knows he has the money, so she goes up there and tries to get it. As soon as he runs low, she'll be too busy to even say hello."

In spite of exploitation between the management, maids, and residents, there is also a degree of caring and help giving by maids for older residents. As a rule, they are aware of the behavioral patterns of residents and notify the management of sickness or irregular behavior. They go out of their way to check on elderly residents and in time have their favorites; some maids provide real services at a reasonable rate of exchange. For example, one maid would sew and mend older persons' clothing for a minimal payment. In some cases, residents wait for maids to make their rounds so they can greet them and spend time in friendly conversation. At the Ballentine, one of the female residents assisted the maids in their rounds. This provided the woman with companionship—an appreciated function—and also kept her abreast of the residents' activities. For older male residents, the maid may be the only woman with whom they interact on a regular basis.

Notes

1   See H.W. Zorbaugh, *The Golden Coast and the Slums* (Chicago: University of Chicago Press, 1926); N.S. Hayner, *Hotel Life* (Asheville, North Carolina: University of North Carolina Press, 1936); A.M. Rose, "Interest in the Living Arrangement of the Urban Unattached," *American Journal of Sociology* 53 (May, 1948).

2   See: J.H. Shapiro, *Communities of the Alone* (New York: Association Press, 1971); P. Ehrlich, *St. Louis' "Invisible" Elderly Needs and Characteristics of Aged "Single Room Occupancy" Downtown Hotel Residents* (St. Louis: Institute of Applied Gerontology, St. Louis University, 1976); B.J. Stephens, *Loners, Losers, and Lovers: Elderly Tenants in a Slum Hotel* (Seattle: University of Washington Press, 1976); H. Siegal, *Outposts of the Forgotten; Lifeways of Socially Terminal People in Slum Hotels and Single Room Occupancy Tenements* (New Jersey: Transaction Books, 1978).

3   H. Gans, *The Urban Villagers* (New York: The Free Press, 1962), p. 143.

4   Formal supports of those given are part of a defined job or social role. Informal supports include the kinds of assistance occurring when hotel staff and others go beyond the formal parameters for their jobs (H.Z. Lopata, "Support Systems of Elderly Urbanities: Chicago of the 1970s," *The Gerontologist* 15, no. 1 (1975): Part 1:35-41.

5   Helen Lopata (Ibid., p. 35) has defined a *support system* as a "set of relationships involving the giving and receiving of objects, services, social and emotional supports defined by the giver and the receiver as necessary or at least as helpful in maintaining a style of life."

6   Shapiro, *Communities.*

7   The pattern of "manager as employee" of the hotel owner or leasee is the most common operating arrangement found in the downtown SRO hotels. In a few small hotels, the owner acts as the manager, but this pattern is rare.

8   In one instance, a pimp and a prostitute lived in the hotel for several months, paying on a daily basis. The room they rented cost over $350 per month. The prostitute was addicted to narcotics, which the pimp supplied and used to control her behavior. The management was aware of the circumstances, yet chose to look the other way and allow what several residents termed "modern day slavery."

9   S. Ryan, "Chambermaids: A Profile of Some Women's Work," *Social Policy* (March/April, 1977):36-37.

10   E. Liebow, *Tally's Corner* (Boston: Little, Brown, 1967), p. 37.

11   Ibid.

6

Caretakers and Exploiters: Agencies and Others

Employees of the federal and state governments along with other service personnel comprise what Boissevain calls the "anonymous service fringe."[1] These are the people who staff service organizations and with whom the older people have relatively frequent contacts, e.g., postal clerks, bank tellers, shopkeepers, employees of Social Security and Welfare offices, etc. Urban dwellers have little personal knowledge about these individuals and have only single-stranded service relationships with them.[2] However, for some older individuals, agencies create a structure for social relationships. D'Arcy, in an analysis of the social networks of downtown hotel residents, found that some older persons attempt to personalize the normally nonpersonal relationships of the service fringe. She notes:

> It may be said, then, that the agencies create the structure for Bob's social relationships. The individuals in the agencies are only performing their assigned duties. And yet, to Bob, these people are not fungible—they are "friends." For example, he receives cash assistance from Welfare and job assistance from the "officer" in the State Rehabilitation Department and O.S.C.A. Thus, apart from the "professor" in the Laundry School who gives him clothes, it is the nonmaterial items of joking behavior and personal attention which are the

important elements of "friendship." Through his social
relations with individuals such as the "professor" and the
"officer" he obtains support to attain his goals.[3]

The anonymous service fringe provides (to older hotel
residents) secondary social supports which encompass a broad
spectrum of behavior. Such supports range from highly
structured and formalized social/health services to informal
helping of a utilitarian and ad hoc nature.

Secondary supports can be described along several
dimensions. Gans's description of "caretaker" exemplifies the
formal aspect of secondary supports:

> It shall refer to agencies and individuals who not only give
> patient care, but other kinds of aid that they think will benefit
> the client, and who offer aid as an end in itself, rather than as
> a means to a more important end. Caretakers thus include
> those people and agencies who offer medical and psychiatric
> treatment, case work, occupational, social, and psychological
> counseling, economic assistance, technical aid or information,
> advice in general, and educational and quasi-educational
> programs intended to benefit their users.[4]

As mentioned above, reciprocity—not altruism—is the
driving force behind formal caretaking relationships. The
caretakers give services in exchange for material and non-
material return. For example, the professionalization of social
services has led to a transformation of services into
"commodities" that are sold to "clients." Repayment, while not
financial, still exists in the form of deference or compliance—
that is, "good" and predictable behavior on the part of the
client. The quantity of services delivered relates directly to the
level of public funds flowing into the organization. Large client
case loads contribute to institutional strength, which in turn
shows that the caretaking agency is performing a valuable
function. The larger the case load, the more public funds can be
requested. Gans points out that the caretaking portion of the
exchange can be oriented in at least three ways:

1) *service oriented* - The caretaker helps the client
   achieve goals that he cannot achieve by himself;

2) *market oriented* - the caretaker gives the client "what he wants," resembling a commercial exchange;

3) *missionary oriented* - the client is expected to adopt the caretaker's own behavior and values.

Each of the above orientations asks that the client adopt a quasi-dependent role vis-a-vis the caretaker. In the last approach, caretakers' expectations can be overt (rescue missions, Alcoholics Anonymous), or subtle (social service organizations that encourage the client to adopt middle-class values and behavior). Some quasi-dependent roles are deemed more "legitimate" than others.

In the United States, dependency on the government to meet one's needs is generally stigmatized; yet dependency upon the private corporation for the means to meet one's needs is encouraged by the free enterprise system. Since dependency on the private sector is valued and legitimized, it is often viewed as a sign of "independence" and "individualism." Several older hotel residents have expressed a similar attitude with regard to veterans' benefits versus MediCal. One man reported, "Veteran's is better than inadequate Medicare benefits. MediCal pays all, but I'd never consider that, I've always paid my way."

Distinctions concerning what constitutes "legitimate" dependencies are culturally determined and affect the self-image of those cast in the recipient role. Cultural imperatives as to what constitutes "legitimate" dependencies force many older persons to make a difficult choice between denial on the one hand and self-recrimination on the other. Collins notes that such cultural values,

> play a crucial role in stigmatizing those, such as the aged or unemployed youth, who are unable to avail themselves of "legitimate" ways of meeting their needs (due to a now systematic oversupply of labor in the labor market) and who must resort to other means of meeting their needs (e.g., welfare or government subsidized old-age pensions) which are often culturally defined as "illegitimate" or as indicating an individual deficiency in the recipient.[5]

The value and structure of these institutions perpetuates the notion that needs result from individual faults rather than societal and institutional deficiencies.

Few persons living in the SRO hotel are employed in full time jobs with any degree of stability. They are susceptible to layoffs and unemployment. Their vulnerability opens them to the plethora of external caretakers serving downtown residents. The following discussion centers on the most visible providers of services to older hotel residents.

The Bureaucracy

Over thirty formal professional social/health agencies and organizations impinge on, or in some way involve themselves with, older persons living in downtown hotels. The majority of these organizations are external caretakers with a service and missionary orientation. The most prominent of the external caretakers are the Social Security Administration and State Department of Public Welfare. Older persons who meet the qualifications are eligible for Supplemental Security Income (SSI) and MediCal from the state in addition to their Social Security. Special services are also available such as counseling and conservatorship in which the person is given assistance in managing personal affairs.

The Social Security and welfare systems confront the older client with a massive and confusing bureaucracy. When faced with the "red tape," older clients react in several ways. Most commonly, they express a frustration or powerlessness to affect the system. They receive their checks, are grateful for what they receive, and leave it at that. The bureaucratic structure so intimidates some persons that they give up despite their eligibility for SSI and other benefits. As one man told me, "I've given up trying to get SSI, it's just too much of a hassle." Others receive their Social Security and view the SSI as a welfare payment, which they won't accept even though they are eligible. Such persons hover at the poverty line and comprise the bulk of older SRO hotel residents.

Another common response is for the older person to become angry and cynical about governmental programs and social services. In one case, an older hotel resident became so enraged with the welfare department that he threatened to shoot his conservator. From his point of view, the welfare department had aided in having his wife institutionalized. He felt that he had little to say about the actions that placed her in a home, and he said the particular home was just interested in her Medicare check. After many frustrating attempts to "free his wife" from the nursing home, he became depressed, consumed more alcohol, and began to deteriorate rapidly. Shortly after I left the field, I received word that he too had been placed in a nursing home.

In general, most older persons react to the federal and state bureaucracies with an indifference tempered by realism. The system is understood to be a "mess," so one must do the best one can to assure "I get what's coming to me."

For some older residents, Social Security and SSI provide a stable source of income which can be manipulated and managed to provide a bearable existence. As one older resident of the Ballentine stated:

> From Las Vegas, I came here, and I'm here the last four years and here they help me more. You know, with the SSI. I told them I was just getting Social Security. I wasn't getting enough money to live on, really. It was too hard a struggle, so they put me on SSI.

In the cases of older residents who could no longer function, the management at the Ballentine would contact a private nonprofit organization focusing specifically on older adults, "who are having difficulty managing their affairs and have no one to act on their behalf." The organization offers "protective services" to older adults who are not receiving help from the Department of Public Welfare or similar public agencies. Individual case workers have a designated turf and spend some portion of their time visiting clients. Overwhelming paper work results in many caseworkers spending less than 50 percent of their time in actual casework. Caseworker-client relationships are sometimes strained from lack of trust as well as social and ethnic dissimilarity. As one resident and "client" of a "protective agency" told me:

> Kevin, I saw _____ yesterday; she can't help me. She's just a kid, might still be in school. I need someone with power to get me through all this.... At least she's better than the Mexican I talked to before.

Social and Health Services

The Veterans Administration influences many of the men living in lower rent hotels. It is truly an external caretaker—its social services are located in a posh shopping and hotel complex several miles from the downtown, and its hospital facilities located in the exclusive area of La Jolla. Because there are no outreach services, downtown residents must exert considerable energy to avail themselves of these services. As with other bureaucratized organizations, the V.A. delivers mass depersonalized care of a sort that often frustrates clients. As shown in this older resident's account, long waits, jargon, and red tape all contribute to the powerlessness felt by many users.

> But old Sam. I've known Sam for two or three years. He's been there twenty-three years (at the hotel). A couple of years since I've been dropping in on him on account of he's alone and it's difficult. He'll be ninety in August. I took him up to the Veterans Hospital, but being ninety years old ... one time we waited four hours and then they just took his blood pressure. Then we waited two more hours and they took his weight. Then we had to come back again. But you know when you're ninety years old that's a strain. And, of course, he didn't get any more attention than anybody that was younger. Like I say, you wait four hours, and you don't dare ... one thing about it, you don't dare leave. If they'd say, well now, we won't call you for four hours, why we could fiddlestick around. But when you wait, you wait every minute—you don't like to go to the washroom for fear that they call you, and if they call you and you're not there, they may not call you before another hour.

The V.A. Hospital and several other hospitals located near the downtown provide the major portion of health services to older hotel residents. The most frequent contacts are with hospital out-patient departments and emergency rooms. Again, the rule is for the older client to receive depersonalized and fragmented care. Since most of the care is sought in crisis situations, emergency room staff take little personal interest in their clients and often negatively stereotype them on the basis of address south of Broadway, clothing, and age. An emergency room nurse in a major hospital told me,

> Oh yeh, we get a lot of "winos" from the skid row hotels downtown. Seems like we get some almost every night. We treat them if they're banged up, but won't admit them—if they're drunk, we won't admit 'em.

The experiences of older hotel residents with hospital care and physician treatment are overwhelmingly negative. An all too common adjustment of many residents is to avoid hospital and doctors altogether. For some, the costs are high since avoidance contributes to the seriousness of health crises when they do occur.

All health services touching the lives of hotel residents are based on the acute-care medical model. There are no preventive health services or intervention strategies available to them. To complicate matters further, people become lost in the maze of referrals. One health official reported that individuals are often admitted to a private hospital located near the downtown and not transferred to other hospitals familiar with their case, because "they want to use up the Medicare and MediCal . . . The people at County hospital wonder where they went."

In some instances, residents adjust and manipulate the health care system to meet their needs. For example, one seventy-eight-year-old man living on Social Security and SSI found that doctors and hospitals could provide backup support when his personal funds ran low. He suffered from several chronic disorders and sporadic drunkenness. Toward the end of the month when he was low on funds and could no longer tolerate spending nights in the Greyhound Bus Station, he would call his doctor and feign illness,

> No need to worry my friend! If I run short (of money), I just call my doctor, Dr. Naper, a wonderful man, and I tell him my legs are ready to give out or that I have an angina attack, and he has me admitted to Paradise hospital.

For most residents at the Ballentine and other downtown hotels, an established relationship with a private physician is a luxury. For those who do have one, it can be a strong motivating force to remain in the area. Some report that they would not move because, "I wouldn't want to lose my doctor. Anyway, fewer doctors take MediCal and Medicare, so I might not be able to get another one."

Out of necessity, some switch to a handful of doctors located in the "skid row" area. One older person reported,

> I'd like to use County hospital's out-patient department. I like using the one in Sacramento, but it's too inconvenient. Instead, I use the Chinese doctor over on Market. I can hardly understand him and I resent the way he talks down to me. I'm an intelligent man and could understand.

Doctors who locate their practices in the area are either old or of foreign birth. Class differences, complicated by technical vocabulary—and in some cases real language barriers—tend to prevent a mutually beneficial client-practitioner relationship. All this "reaffirms" what clients already "know"—doctors and hospitals should be avoided. "They're just out for the Medicare buck," or "I'd rather die in the hotel than let them cut, jab, and poke at me."

Some social/health caretakers provide exceptional care on an individual basis. They might be associated with a community center, local government department or religious service organization. One individual (and the only one) providing public health services to residents of the entire downtown expressed frustration when faced with an ineffective and complex social service system.

I try to do something and not become part of the problem. Referrals to some other agencies are a problem and they are just not effective. _____ still hasn't helped the last person I referred to them. It's a jungle out there. Agencies fight over cases. They always want to know why a case wasn't referred to them. There is a lot of jealousy. Everybody wants their pet project to be funded . . . . The Health Department is just not aware of the need and the hotels are scary places for women. The Wells Fargo Hotel, I hate it. There should be male nurses who go there. Anyway, you can't solve everybody's problem. I can help some people some of the time. You need to reserve strength to help those who will help themselves.

Some organizations, despite their location in the downtown area, fail to reach older persons living in the lower rent hotels south of Broadway. The "senior centers" are outgrowths of a movement started thirty-five years ago in New York. As of 1970, the number of senior centers exceeded 1,200. The original emphasis of the senior center movement was to provide opportunities and facilities for recreational roles. The early emphasis on recreation has been supplemented by useful service components including legal aid, medical care, and information and referral services. However, the social component of the centers is still recreation and "entertainment." Unfortunately, these roles become biased to the middle class and fail to provide substantive roles such as work and parenting that many older persons value. In short, "recreational" roles and activities are geared to middle-class cultural norms and fail as adequate substitutes for employment and other roles.

Interviewer: Morton, do you go up to the senior center?

Respondent: What do I want to go there for? I've been up there; just a bunch of old ladies. What could they do for me? I go to the V.A. if I need anything. Anyway, that kind of thing is not for me—I don't dance. Even if I could, I wouldn't walk that far . . . .

Each of the centers providing services to older persons is located north of Broadway in the "higher class" business and

residential area. For many older residents living south of
Broadway, the single-factor of location creates an invisible
boundary curtailing their participation. A manager of a lower
rent hotel south of Broadway summed it up:

> They talk about senior citizens having publications and
> everything else . . . this is going to happen, that's going to
> happen. I don't think that in this area that one out of ten of
> the senior citizens ever find out about something that's being
> sponsored for them until after it's over.

The most visible service-oriented caretakers in the
downtown are the *police*. As is the case in other lower class
groups and communities, the police are expected to provide a
wide range of services. They are looked to in times of trouble,
crisis, and indecision.[6] For example, hotel managers and staff
utilize the police to control residents, and to aid in emergency
medical situations involving illness and death.

Older persons living in the hotels usually come in
contact with the police only in crisis situations. Police
ambulances provide transportation when they are severely ill.
However, police assist only in clear emergency situations. A
desk clerk reported,

> The police will not come unless they're on their death bed. It
> has to be a definite emergency. So many end up hiring a
> private ambulance—I don't know who pays for that.

The procedures taken when someone dies in the hotel always
involve the police. Many managers and hotel staff told us about
deaths in hotels. The following is a policeman's account of such
an incident, taken from a recent newspaper article:

> "Old people," says Vattimo, "the only way you know they're
> dead is by the smell." This hotel is better than most
> downtown. The hallways are lit, at least. The stench creeps
> up on you, like half waking up in the middle of the night to
> find a three-inch cockroach beating a shortcut path across
> your chest. "There's no smell in the world like the smell of
> dead people," the recruit is saying . . . . His skin is ready to
> burst into a billion particles, but he's trying hard to be a
> solemn, no-nonsense cop. From the hallway you can see the

old man on the floor, spider legs sticking out from a huge belly. The bed blocks his face from view. "You don't want to see his face," the kid says. "He's foaming at the mouth." It's sort of internal combustion, Vattimo explains. After a body has lain closeted-up for a couple of days, as this man's body has, the insides burst out from the mouth.[7]

Police assistance is variable and not always in the interest of the client. At another hotel, a desk clerk related an instance in which a man was disoriented and frequently fell down in his room. The police were summoned as a last resort, but provided no assistance. This particular example also illustrates the way in which some hotel residents care for one another and the kinds of dilemmas they fear.

But the thing is you *don't know who to call.* Like I say, lot of 'em [older residents] don't want to go and ... some of the clerks that run the places—they don't want to be involved. They would call the police. But I know of a case where the police went up there and asked the man if he could walk, and he said no and so the police went down, got in the car, and went away. I'll tell you what happened. I went up there with a wheel chair and got him in the wheel chair and took a cab and took him to the ... I forget whether it was the hospital or the clinic. But I don't like to take that on because sometimes at the hospital if you sign the paper, why you're hooked. I have got the money to pay it, but I still don't like to invite that trouble. It seems as though around here you get kind of kind-hearted and you're in trouble. You just hate to leave 'em.

The inconsistency with which police handle older adults living in downtown hotels relates to their negative attitudes about such persons. The police, because of their frequent contacts with the "winos," street people, pimps and prostitutes, tend to lump all hotel residents together as part of the "seamy element." On the basis of newspaper articles, and discussion with the police and other "public servants" there is little appreciation or understanding of the invisible majority of "respectable" older persons living in the lower rent hotels south of Broadway.

Some portion of older persons with drinking problems came in contact with *Detox*, the slang term for "Detoxification

Center," an alcoholic treatment center located in the downtown. Detox views alcoholism as a medical problem requiring treatment and care. Police no longer take "drunks" to the County Jail, but instead deposit them at Detox. However, Detox requires an involved intake procedure similar to being "booked" into jail. It also requires that persons give up their clothes and wear hospital-type gowns. Treatment can last from several days to several weeks. While an improvement over the County Jail, Detox is established on the acute care medical model. It provides no outreach into the hotels, thus no preventive care.

Store owners and bartenders have been described as caretakers in ethnic and working-class neighborhoods.[8] Similarly, caretakers south of Broadway include restaurant waitresses, bartenders, and a myriad of small shop owners.

Bartenders performed both a control and care function for a small portion of older hotel residents. Their most important functions are "looking after" a person who has had too much to drink and listening to "problems." One woman reported to me how special the bartender made her feel: "He keeps a special gallon of wine for me, and looks after me and lets me know when I've had enough. I always know 'cause he starts telling me to switch to grape juice." For some, bars help "break the boredom" and allow for social interaction.

The "Barber College" and the many small shops offered needed services to many older hotel residents. At the Barber College, there are over a dozen men and women enrolled in a one-year course of training. The "College" offers haircuts for $1.00 and shaves for $.50. When business is slow some persons receive a haircut and shave free. One student told me about her older clients:

> Well, this one guy has been coming in for a shave, face massage, and haircut ever since I started here. Sometimes he comes in three times a week for the face massage. We talk a lot, he tells me about his room and the things that happen down here. I really like it here, I mean, I might even try to work in a shop down here after I graduate. Anyway, I think I'm the only one that ever touches some of these guys. It's probably the closest they ever get to a woman.

At one liquor store, I discovered a unique relationship between two young clerks and an old man. The old man looked to the store keepers for companionship, advice, and occasional loans. The young clerks admired the man for being a "fighter." They felt he drank too much so offered control functions when necessary: "We ration how much we sell him, if he seems really bad, we'll make him stay here till we close then run him back to the hotel." The old man was able to obtain companionship and some "extra money" through his affiliation with the store. In order to make extra money, he placed himself outside the store and assisted under-aged sailors and street people in purchasing beer and whiskey. For this, he received a percentage of the purchase. His function aided the liquor store business while at the same time protecting the clerks from making sales to minors. Additionally, the older man, because of his multiple ailments and access to medication, supplied one of the clerks with various prescription medications in exchange for "Ancient Age" whiskey and cash.

The preceding two chapters have considered the caretaking and occasionally the exploiting behaviors of persons, organizations, and agencies located both inside and outside the hotel environment. The services available to older hotel dwellers are numerous, yet they use only those services deemed necessary for everyday survival. The services provided by the hotel staff—housekeeping, someone to call in an emergency, etc.—are extremely important for the well-being of the older residents. The next chapter explores the major social divisions within the SRO hotel and the nature of relationships among residents.

Notes

1   J. Boissevain, *Friend of Friends: Networks, Manipulators, and Coalitions* (Oxford: Basil Blackwell, 1974), p. 123.

2   A social relationship between two people based on a single role relation. A relation that covers many roles is termed multiplex or many-stranded (Ibid., p. 30).

3   A.M. D'Arcy, "Elderly Hotel Residents and Their Social Networks in Downtown San Diego," Masters Thesis, San Diego State University, 1976.

4   H. Gans, *The Urban Villagers* (New York: The Free Press, 1962), p. 142.

5   C.J.L. Collins, *Social Service Needs of the Aged. Social and Rehabilitation Services* (Washington, D.C.: United States Department of Health, 1972), p. 124.

6   A.J. Reiss, Jr. *The Police and the Public* (New Haven: Yale University Press, 1971).

7   *The Sentinel* (San Diego), 1977, 6-a.

8   Gans, *Urban Villagers,* p. 160.

7

The Social World of the SRO

The previous chapter explored the boundaries and
social division between hotel staff and tenants and between
social agencies and tenants. This chapter explores the social
groupings found among the tenants themselves. Attention is also
directed at the characteristics of the older SRO residents'
relationships to kinsmen.

Transients and Permanents

Among SRO tenants, there are several distinctions. The
most obvious was briefly considered in Chapter 5, the division
between transients and permanents. Transients are those
individuals who have lived in the Ballentine for six months or
less, pay on a daily or weekly basis, and look at the hotel as
temporary housing. Several other factors contribute to the
residents' distinction between permanent and transient. In the
Ballentine, age is the most obvious characteristic. Younger
individuals, even those who have lived in the hotel for a year or
more, are not referred to as permanents. The feeling is that such
persons are only temporarily living in the hotel for purposes of
their job or until they "get on their feet." Unlike the older
permanents, the younger people are expected to move on.

Between the transients and permanents, there is a great

social distance. In spite of their close spatial proximity, they have little to do with one another. The boundaries separating their social worlds are sharp and few social relationships develop across them.

Older permanents view the transients as intruders, and say it is largely they who are responsible for trouble in the hotel. The increase in the number of transient residents makes the hotel a less satisfactory living environment for the older residents. They see transients as irresponsible in their actions and condemn them for their attitudes toward the hotel.

Many younger transient tenants are unemployed or on welfare. This fact increases the resentment of permanents for transients. Older permanents refer to them as "welfare bums" or "hippies" and view their "aimlessness" as inexcusable. Most of the older permanents feel they have worked hard for their small pensions and social security. Many still would like to be working. Thus, they have little sympathy for younger persons on welfare. Their summation is, "They could work if they wanted to."

As reported by an older permanent,

> The young ones come and go — some for a day, week, or even a month or two. They smoke marijuana, I know that smell, and sit around doing nothing, just taking up space in the T.V. room. There was one guy who was so much on drugs that he'd wander into my room or just stand at the door in a daze. I'd tell 'im to get out.

Older permanent residents are dependent on the public areas of the hotel for expanding their social space beyond the confines of their rooms. A factor of concern and aggravation for permanent residents is the intrusion of younger transients into the lobby and T.V. areas of the hotel. The common pattern is for transients not to use the public areas of the hotel. However, this is changing at the Ballentine. The change began when a young drug-dependent couple moved into the hotel, after which a group of young street people began to congregate in the lobby and T.V. room. This development was viewed negatively by older permanents who called it a "take over" and cited it as additional proof of the lowering standard in the hotel.

Similar shifts in the age composition of the hotel population are reported in other hotels. A former clerk at the Wells Fargo Hotel expressed concern at changes taking place there, and the problems that arise when young and old tenants live in close proximity.

> . . . I don't see the mix where the balance of power changes, because I don't think it is feasible any more to have eighteen to twenty-year-old boys out of the county jail in there with old men who obviously have money hidden around in their rooms. I think the—well, what is the old saying? A thief without an opportunity to steal considers himself an honest man. As a rule, you have to have security, and if you let down on security, you are inviting trouble. I don't see it as a mixed deal. Because I had a few incidents in there where the young punks would say, "Get back in your room, old man, and shut up." You know, I'm not the youngest man in the room anymore, and that puts me in a black mood. When they show no respect for the old man, I can't have any for them. Those old men are very generous if they can just find a winner when they bet at the racetrack.

In short, older residents view the young transient as distinctly different from themselves. Differences in age, values, and attitudes toward the hotel combine to minimize the degree of social interaction between transients and permanents.

Men and Women

A distinguishing feature of SRO hotels in San Diego and elsewhere is the great proportion of older males. SRO hotels are one of the few living environments for older persons where the trend for older women to outnumber older men is reversed. In contrast, middle class hotels have a more nearly equal distribution of males to females and differ in social patterning.[1] In part, the increase of women in middle-class hotels relates to the fact that most of the hotels are located outside the "tenderloin" zone. Women are typically found in apartment arrangements or single family dwellings with cooking facilities. They are less likely to choose the SRO hotel as a living environment.

Ten women live in the Ballentine Hotel on a permanent basis. Four of the women have lived in the hotel for over ten years; they are old and unemployed. Three of those four worked in the downtown area as waitresses and hotel maids before "retiring." As a group, the women view the hotel as home and prefer it over other living arrangements. One woman stated her reason for selecting the hotel over an apartment:

> The advantages are that you have a lot of people. If you get tired of staying in your room, you can go to the lobby, then back to your room. I don't like apartments because here if you get sick or anything happens you get help right away. If you live in an apartment by yourself, you can drop dead and no one will know the difference. That's what I like about living here. I can get help right away if something happens, which is good health-wise.

The supportive aspect of hotel life is expressed by both older men and women residents. Living in the hotel provides them with a ready and available helping network. For many older residents, living in a hotel is an adaptive strategy providing benefits over and above other living environments.

The dominant values of self-reliance, freedom, and privacy are exemplified by SRO women no less than men. This particular finding contradicts what Stephens found in a Detroit SRO hotel. She found that women had a reduced capacity to cope, a greater vulnerability, and were even more isolated and lonely than were the men. Most critically, they were deficient in the important area of independence.[2]

Data from San Diego SROs indicate that women are more likely than men to be involved in social networks and supportive arrangements. Since the SRO is a predominantly male environment, even if women are more dependent than men, they have a large pool of older men from which they can select relationships. While the normative pattern in the SRO is to avoid intimacy and binding relationships, women are able to work out symbiotic relationships with other women and, in some cases, with male residents.

Elderly women living in the SRO are not newcomers to

the setting. They have lived and worked in such settings for the larger part of their lives. Some have led conventional lives, have been married and raised children. Even if they were married at one time, most have worked all their lives and feel a sense of independence and ability to "make it" without a man.

In the Ballentine, women are the central nodes in groups that form between residents. In hotels where there are even fewer women than in the Ballentine, group formation among residents is conspicuously absent, except those based on gambling.

One of the few networks of neighbors I found in the downtown SRO hotels centers around several female residents living in the Ballentine Hotel. This group involves six permanent residents and is dependent on two women, Linda and Harriet, both of whom have lived in the hotel for many years. The women frequently visit with each other and have two separate clusters of men whom they visit. A cluster of friends does not necessarily mean that each member actively neighbors with the other. Aside from each other, Harriet and Linda visit on a reciprocal basis only with their boyfriends. In addition, each woman has individual male acquaintances whom she "helps." These are not reciprocal neighboring patterns, but instead unidirectional—the women go to the friends' rooms to visit and provide assistance (see Figure 1).

Neighboring, as in the case of this group, or calling on the room telephone is crucial for information flow within the hotel, especially among acquaintances. Desk clerks are involved in the communication/gossip network since they operate the telephone switchboard. In this way some desk clerks become informal members of the specific groups and are often expected to have certain kinds of information. For example, Dave, an older paraplegic who had lived in the hotel for thirteen years, would call me each morning to ask if his friend Harriet had left the hotel. If she had not left, he would ask for me to ring her room. When Harriet left the hotel, she would leave a message for Dave as to where she was going and when she would return.

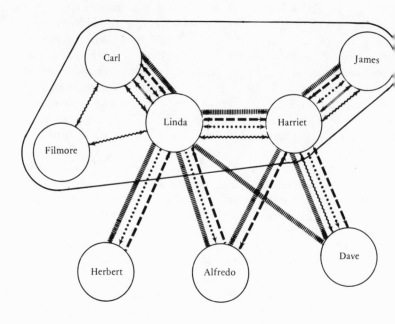

Relational Content: Arrow represents flow of transaction
reciprocal transactions represented by
double arrow

——————————   Activity cluster

••••••••••••   Neighboring

— — — —   Money or material goods

||||||||||||||||||||||||| Aid (Medical, Food, Running errands)

|||||||||||||||||||||| Sexual

〜〜〜〜〜〜   Telephone

Figure 1

Social Group

Thus, the desk clerk knows a lot about residents and was often entrusted with information to relay to other persons.

There were several instances in which a desk clerk's failure to notify someone of sickness or injury was considered bad faith. For example, one evening Dave fell while taking a shower. He managed to struggle to the elevator and ring for the desk clerk. The clerk found him with a large gash on his forehead and sent for an ambulance at his request. The next morning Harriet discovered what had happened to Dave and was upset because she had not been notified immediately.

In another instance, an eighty-six-year-old resident named Alfredo became very ill during my shift as night clerk. He was so ill that I called a police ambulance and had him taken to the hospital. In the morning, when my shift ended, I reported the incident to the hotel manager. The next night when I came on duty, Linda was waiting for me. She was angry because I had not called her the previous night when Alfredo became ill. She felt that I should have notified her first. To make matters worse, the manager on day shift had not told her about Alfredo being taken to the hospital. Instead, she heard about Alfredo through the gossip network—she viewed this as a real insult to her long-term friendship with Alfredo.

A unique feature of the social network, illustrated in Figure 1, is the regular and ritualized activity of dressing up and going to dinner each Sunday afternoon. This is one of the very few instances in which hotel residents get together outside of the hotel to do things. In general, residents of SRO hotels resist getting together (outside the hotel) with other residents.

Another interesting feature of this group is the relationship between Linda and Harriet. Both have lived in the hotel for over fifteen years, and both depend upon each other for help in times of illness. They also do such favors as telling the other about special sales, or picking up things at the store. In spite of their apparent friendship, Linda is adamant about not referring to Harriet as a "friend." For her, Harriet is an "acquaintance," a person who can be relied on for assistance, but *not* someone to confide in. In conversations, Linda refers to

Harriet in negative terms. She does not respect her for numerous reasons, ranging from a belief that she is a chronic liar to a resentment of her accepting Supplemental Security Income (SSI). In reference to Harriet, Linda once told me,

> I *hate* Harriet. She's a liar and nosy as hell, but she helps me when I'm sick. When I broke my arm she helped me dress and took care of business, and I do the same for her . . . . It burns me up that she makes over $40.00 a month more than me. She's on SSI, you know, that welfare. People on welfare do better than me. I just don't understand that.

The relationship between Linda and Harriet exemplifies the utilitarian and practical features of social relationships among older hotel dwellers.

While the men involved in the activity cluster centering around Linda and Harriet know one another, they have only minimal social interaction outside of their weekly dinner trips and fleeting conversations in the public areas of the hotel.

Two other social groupings in the Ballentine have one woman, Alice, as the key member. Alice is referred to by the manager as "Florence Nightingale" since both groups depended on her willingness to be "helpful." Alice is a longtime hotel resident. Before retiring at sixty, she worked as a waitress in the downtown area. She has never married and refused to discuss the death of a man whom she had intended to marry some thirty years earlier.

Alice is a full-time "helper." She acts on a power of attorney and looks after Beatrice, an eighty-year-old woman suffering from memory loss. Together they form a pseudofamilial mother-daughter dyad. In addition to relying on Alice, Beatrice has a male friend, Winston, with whom she is a steady companion. Together, Alice, Beatrice, and Winston form a group that dominates the T.V. room each evening.

Each evening shortly before 7:00, they arrive in the T.V. room armed with the "guide" *(T.V. Guide)* and seat themselves on "their" sofa. Their arrival in the T.V. room is planned so that they get there before other residents. They select "their" channel and settle in for the evening.

Winston, the male member of the group, is seventy-eight years old and has lived in the hotel for three years. The relationship between Beatrice and him might best be described as a "helping pair" based on their special needs. Neither is married. They met in the hotel. During the waking hours, they spend all their time together helping one another with walking, providing companionship, and security. Beatrice is forgetful and has, on several occasions, got lost outside the hotel late at night. With Winston at her side, this problem is decreased. Although Winston is more mentally alert, he has real dependency needs for companionship. As a helping pair, both can have their needs met while maintaining a semblance of independence.

Alice is also a pseudomember of a group of alcoholic men living in the Ballentine.[3] Her primary function in the group is that of nurturing mother. When members of the group are too drunk to care for themselves, Alice goes to their rooms, sits with them, cleans them up, and feeds them. She is not an alcoholic and scolds the men for their behavior. Although she disapproves of their drinking, the men know that she can be relied on for "help." They respect her and in conversation refer to her as "a lady with a lot of class."

Over a several month period of time, Alice developed a relationship with one member of the group. As this occurred, she became less concerned with caring for other members of the group and focused more attention on her new "boyfriend." In the following months, the group dissolved as a result of Shelly's hard-nosed policies toward alcoholics. The configuration of Alice's helping network is illustrated in Figure 2.

Not all women in the Ballentine are involved in social groups. Two women, both discharged from state mental hospitals, are among the most isolated residents of the hotel. During my tenure at the hotel, I never saw either of them interact with any other residents, or use the lobby or the T.V. room. They remained in their rooms continually, leaving only for meals.

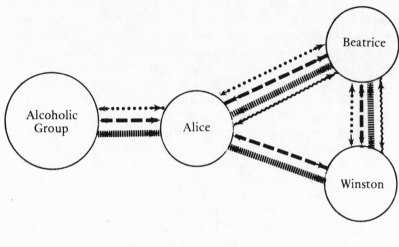

Relational Content: Arrow represents flow of transaction
reciprocal transactions represented by
double arrow

——————————	Activity cluster
••••••••••••••	Neighboring
– – – – – – –	Money or material goods
▐▐▐▐▐▐▐▐▐▐▐	Aid (Medical, Food, Running errands)
▏▏▏▏▏▏▏▏▏▏▏▏	Sexual
∿∿∿∿∿∿∿∿	Telephone

Figure 2
Alice's Helping Network

The most prominent all-male group in the Ballentine centers around several older permanents who regularly meet in the hotel lobby during afternoon and evening hours. The management referred to the group as the "lobby lizards." Their pattern is to sit together and discuss politics, sports, gambling, or sex. Their association is limited to the lobby and does not carry over into activities outside the hotel. While two regular members of the group are involved in betting and playing cards, these activities are done outside the hotel, not with hotel residents.

In general, the interactions between women living in the hotels are similar to those found among men. They are characterized by a lack of trust and a superficiality in content. Women, like men, are "tough" and suspicious of others knowing too much about them. The value they place on their freedom and privacy minimizes the formation of confidant relationships. The most striking feature of all relationships is their utilitarian and practical content.

The most important aspect of a relationship is its utility in times of personal need.

Dimensions of Relationships among Hotel Residents

As a means of exploring the characteristics of relationships among older hotel residents in downtown, a group of forty-three randomly selected SRO hotel residents who responded to health questions to be reported in Chapter 9 were also asked to name three friends and say what it was about that friend they liked the most. This question was designed to get at the quality or substance of friendship relationships. The friendships among SRO residents were classified into eighteen dimensions, which in turn grouped into six logical domains or broad categories (see Table 4). These broad domains are similar to those discovered by Lowenthal.[4] The variety of aspects of friendship derive from the respondents' subjective description of their real friends.

Table 4

Domains and Dimensions of Relationships

Domains and Dimensions	No. Persons Mentioning Trait	% of Total Responses
Similarity		
Shared experiences	3	
Sharing activities	7	
Verbal communication	9	
Similar general behavior	5	
Similar interests	5	
Total	29	19
Reciprocity		
Supportive/dependable	28	
Understanding/accepting	9	
Confidant	1	
Trustworthy	15	
Total	53	35
Compatibility		
Likeability	27	
Enjoyment	3	
Total	30	20
Time and Space		
Proximity	2	
Total	12	8
Role Model		
Respecting	12	
Learning/advice	3	
Total	15	10
Other		
Personality	9	
"Just good friends"	1	
Other	3	
Total	13	8
Total Responses	152	100

The most important broad category for the SRO hotel residents centered on *reciprocity*—the quality of being helpful and supportive. Of the 152 descriptive responses covering aspects of friends, 53 or 35 percent centered on this general category. A supportive and dependable type of relationship was the most often sought out and described. In most cases respondents focused on the *utilitarian* nature of the relationship and the benefits they derived from it, rather than its nurturing aspect. Mutuality in the relationship was not often mentioned. Respondents gave direct and concrete descriptions: "He will give me money without any bullshit." or "I can depend on them (hotel management); if I can get to my phone, they're up here in two seconds flat."

A second dimension of reciprocity referred to the understanding and accepting nature of the friend. This aspect was important to 16 percent of those responding in the reciprocity domain. Comments included: "He is very understanding" or "we understand each other." Describing a friend as a confidant was limited to only one respondent. The response was explicit, "He is honest, will not tell other people private things. Will help others when he can." The tendency for hotel residents not to describe friends as confidants supports Ehrlich's finding that the emotional well-being of this population is not directly related either to self-disclosure, or to a confidant relationship.[5] However, this does not mean that the population is not gregarious.

Trustworthiness (honesty) was mentioned sixteen times as an important aspect of friendship. Again these descriptions were direct and to the point, "We trust each other," "Trustworthy," "Trust," or in one case, "He is different from other drunks, and he is honest." As Lowenthal and her associates point out, the domain of reciprocity is probably the most complex, and involves a higher degree of commitment and understanding than the others.[6] For the present study, the label reciprocity proved misleading, since many of those who mentioned that they received help and support did not mention that they returned it. Thus, the domain had a distinctively utilitarian flavor rather than one in which individuals were mutually sharing their private selves.

The second most important domain of friendship was *compatibility,* which accounted for 20 percent of all responses. Emphasis was on the likeability and comfort and ease of relationships. Aspects most mentioned were sociability, niceness, kindness, enjoyment or fun, and friendliness. Responses included, "He's easygoing, a friendly feller" or "He's a good man and tries to be nice."

Similarity was the next most important category for characterizing the qualities of friendship and accounted for 19 percent of the total responses. This domain included five dimensions, all having to do with commonalities in behavior and interest. Ease of verbal communication was the most important dimension within the category. A sense of similarity was reflected in statements like: "We like the races and to talk about the same things," "I just like to talk to him, he has traveled a lot," or simply, "We can communicate with each other." Sharing activities, coupled with shared communication, fostered a sense of similarity: "He is a hard core talker, I like him. Works at the YMCA and we go to UFO meetings together." Or, "He's a fellow drinker and pool player." Shared experiences was another dimension fostering similarity: "He's a good country boy, like me" or "He's quite like me." A few persons mentioned shared behavior as an aspect of their relationship: "He's a fellow bar fly," or "Quiet, like me."

The *role-modeling* type of relationship emphasized attributes to which the respondents themselves aspired and respected: for example, "I respect his stamina and determination to live through a severe heart operation," "He's a very wealthy man, but has tolerance for everybody. He's as common as an ordinary man." Or, "She is a business lady and gets along with all her customers." Several respondents focused on a learning or advice-giving function of friendship: "He gives me that boot in the pants I need. Encouragement and wit." Or, "Telling me off when I mess up."

Next followed a catch-all category including

miscellaneous attributes such as personality characteristics and other responses hard to classify: e.g., "We never have no trouble," "Just a natural friend you don't have to do anything to keep ... don't have to buy a friend." Or, "He comes and sees how I am doing."

The last area of importance in describing friends, time and space dimensions, accounted for 8 percent of the total responses. This category focused on nonsubstantive aspects of the relationship, such as duration of the relationship and geographic proximity. Duration of the relationship accounts for over half of the responses in this domain and included comments like, "I've known him since I moved here four years ago." Proximity or geographic convenience was mentioned by only two persons as an important aspect of friendship. In some other studies, proximity was found to be an important quality of friendship, particularly for the working-class poor and the aged.[7] Since our sample was of similar economic status, but not as old, our data do not directly contradict the findings of the works cited. Our findings do suggest that proximity is not a very important factor in friendships among old, poor hotel residents. Instead, proximity is important for the establishment of utilitarian relationships better described as "acquaintances."

The percentage of no-responses increased as we inquired about second and third friends. Over half of the respondents were unable to respond when asked about the qualities they valued in a third friend. This fact suggests that while older persons in the hotels know and appreciate friendly interaction with a lot of other persons, those considered intimate friends are few in number.[8] The relationships found among downtown hotel residents are best seen as acquaintances or as friendly interactions. Seven of the forty-three persons interviewed said that they had *no* friends.

Kinship

The majority of persons living in the Ballentine say they get little help and have only infrequent contact with relatives. In a large number of cases, persons have not seen relatives for long periods of time. Although there were many reasons for so little contact with kin, several themes emerge. First, some persons have simply outlived their kin. They are the only ones still alive in their family. As one man put it, "I've outlived everybody. My sister died two years ago, so that makes me the last one." Another theme centered on self- or kin-imposed isolation and alienation. In some cases, persons have become alienated from their families as a result of problem drinking and alcoholism. The case of Sammy Hinkle illustrates the destructiveness of problem drinking. In his opinion, alcohol, "has ruined my life. Even though I've been off the sauce now for three years, my brother still won't trust me. He tried to help me several years back, but I blew it."

Many of the persons living in hotels have long since burned out their relationships with relatives. A hotel manager reported the case of a woman who had lived for various lengths of time in several downtown hotels, was well known in the area, yet alienated from family.

> Gertie, she'd come into the bar where I'm working now. She was the town clown or the town character or whatever you want to call her. She weighed seventy-four pounds and stood maybe 4 feet 11 or 5 feet. She had been beautiful twenty years ago. I'd seen pictures of her and she probably was the prettiest woman in the whole downtown area. She'd worked all the bars down here. She was a barmaid and whatever. She had two children and her family disowned her years ago. She lived on her disability check from welfare and her social, you know, some type of—she'd had operations. She had gall bladder trouble. You name it, she had cirrhosis of the liver, the whole bit. She drank booze like it was water, but had a clear mind. She could tell you stories. She'd get everybody laughing and happy. You never asked her, "How you doing today, Gertie?" 'cause she'd tell you, "rotten" but you know if you kept it on a light tone she'd stay light.

After Gertie died, her family came downtown and talked with one of her bartender friends.

> Her family—her mother, her daughter and her son _____ came down and told the bartender next door that knew Gertie quite well that they hadn't wanted to know

or have anything to do with her when she was alive and they didn't want to have anything to do with her now that she was dead. So she was buried in Potter's Field in a pauper's grave. She was a grand lady.

The story of alienation from family is rife among hotel dwellers. Many of the alienated, especially if they are still drinking, are in the worst mental and physical health. They perceive themselves to be isolated, have low morale, and are generally pessimistic about their life situation.

Kinsmen are especially peripheral to the group that classified themselves as "loners." The Ballentine and other SRO hotels have a large number of this kind of person. As one man put it,

> They're loners and no matter where they went to ... I don't care what city they were in, they're still going to be loners. But then they might find the right person that they'd like to talk to, you know, there are people that they talk to, one or two people, and that's their limit of conversation.

Conversation with a man living in another SRO hotel further illustrated the alone pattern of life.

> ... These loners are miserable old bastards. They don't talk to no one, not even their kids. I remember one old Polack who lived here; always kept to himself until another one like him moved in. Well, they hit it off—went everywhere together. After a few months, the new guy moved out. Well, the old man was lost—just wandered around in a daze.

Many of the group characterizing themselves as "loners" report traumatic and stress-filled childhoods. As a group, they left home early in life, reported that they and their parents were hit hard by the Depression, adopted early the lone wolf pattern of living, and said they liked it. Many have never married. Those who did marry divorced early in life. Their work careers are mobile and have been lived in masculine settings— they have been in such 6- brushes with the law. Some of this group have real disabilities and handicaps, both mental and physical. Some of the injuries and disabilities are related to the hazardous and physically demanding jobs open to them. There are two extremes in this group: those with severe health problems, and those who perceive themselves to be in robust health.

Some persons try to avoid contact with kin either because they have something to hide or because they choose not to follow conventional values or the demands of other people. For example, one man, who was married, had left his wife and moved into the Ballentine. He did this after they sold their house and moved into a mobile home. He told me, "Christ, there was no room—and then she went on a health food kick." The reduction in living space, coupled with pressure to change his diet and eating habits, forced a split. He loved to eat and the downtown provided him with a choice of restaurants. In addition, he had facilities in his room for cooking food—a refrigerator, hot plate, toaster broiler, and coffeepot. During a sickness episode, kinsmen made an effort to have him moved into an especially prepared cottage on their property in the northern part of the state. He flatly opposed the plan and pledged that he "wanted to remain in the hotel and intended to die there."

The valued norms are self-reliance, independence, maintenance of privacy, and freedom. The maintenance of self-reliance and independence is directly related to the kinds of nonpersonal formal and informal support systems found in the hotels. As D'Arcy suggests, residents of the lower rent hotels tend to personalize their institutional relationships,

> foraging for friends in the places that fulfill basic needs . . . .
> In other words, the hotel managers, clerks, and others who serve the public are vital individuals in terms of both services and sociability to the elderly occupants of downtown hotels, particularly the SRO.[9]

In summary, primary support systems involving kinsmen are underdeveloped among older persons living in lower rent hotels. Friendship is most frequently defined in utilitarian terms. Few persons mentioned a confidant relationship involving a disclosure of self. Neighboring and helping relationships are found in some hotels. Such arrangements develop among the longtime residents and are most commonly organized around women. Going along with the fact that women are scarce in the SRO hotels, neighboring networks and arrangements are relatively uncommon. Relationships with kinsmen are not strong and few older residents say they rely on them in crisis situations.

Notes

1   R.J. Erickson and J.K. Eckert, "The Elderly Poor in Downtown San Diego Hotels," *The Gerontologist*, 17, no. 5 (October, 1977).

2   B.J. Stephens, *Loners, Losers and Lovers: Elderly Tenants in a Slum Hotel* (Seattle: University of Washington Press, 1976), p. 79.

3   The Ballentine group is in some ways similar to the "matriarchal quasi-family" found by Shapiro (1971) in New York City tenement hotels. In describing the quasi-family she states: "...the dominant woman tends to feed, protect, punish and set norms for the alcoholic 'family' members. They share some meals, and the room of the leader is a hub of continuous social activity.... The matriarch, herself usually an alcoholic, has much power to dictate both the behavior of the family members and their relationships to each other" *(Communities of the Alone*, New York: Association Press, 1971, p. 25).

4   M.F. Lowenthal and B. Robinson, "Social Networks and Isolation," in *Handbook of Aging and the Social Sciences*, ed. R.H. Binstock and E. Shanas (New York: Van Nostrand Reinhold Company, 1976).

5   P. Ehrlich, *St. Louis' "Invisible" Elderly Needs and Characteristics of Aged "Single Room Occupancy" Downtown Hotel Residents* (St. Louis: Institute of Applied Gerontology, St. Louis University, 1976), p. 23.

6   Lowenthal and Robinson, "Social Networks," p. 55.

7   I. Rosow, *Social Integration of the Aged* (New York: Free Press, 1967); G.S. Rosenberg, *The Worker Grows Old: Poverty and Isolation in the City* (San Francisco: Jossey-Bass, 1970).

8   Lowenthal and Robinson ("Social Networks," p. 48) distinguish between at least four types of dyadic relationships: (1) acquaintanceship, (2) friendly interaction, (3) friendship, and (4) intimacy. Each of these types is distinguished by an increment of knowledge about the individuality of the other person, as contrasted with a role-reliant or stereotyped conception. Thus, friendship is more personal and less role-reliant than either friendly interaction or acquaintanceship. The intimate relationship is even more personal and is characterized by closeness, spontaneous interaction, emotional commitment, responsibility and mutuality.

9   A.M. D'Arcy, "Elderly Hotel Residents and Their Social Networks in Downtown San Diego," Masters Thesis, San Diego State University, 1976.

8

Economic Restraints, Dominant Values and Modes of Adjustment

Certain features of the SRO hotel and the downtown environment join together to reinforce the kinds of interpersonal relationships and support systems found among older hotel residents. Primary among these features are economic realities and dominant values and norms—self-reliance, fear of dependency, privacy, and freedom. The single most important mode of adjustment made by the older retiree is the decision to live in the SRO hotel. In the context of the Ballentine and other lower rent hotels, older persons feel a sense of economic independence—they are "paying their own way," thus not becoming overtly dependent on kith, kin, or society. As one older male living in the Ballentine reported to me, "I've found happiness in freedom. I don't answer to nobody. I can go and do what I want and don't have to worry."

Making It Alone

Older persons in the United States suffer acutely from poverty. The older persons living in the SRO hotels are near the bottom of the economic heap. However, despite their minimal fixed incomes and problems, they report that they are getting along pretty well. As long as they can continue to live in "cheap" hotels that make few demands on them and in an area that offers a selection of "cheap" restaurants, they can continue to "make it."

Francis Hsu has proposed that *self-reliance* (and its persistent psychological expression *fear of dependence*) is the core American value.[1] From it emanate the ideals of self-mastery, freedom, etc. Fear of dependency is often so great that those who are overtly dependent, economically or emotionally, are labelled misfits. Furthermore, some forms of dependency (welfare, dependency of adults on their parents) are deemed less appropriate than others.

Perceiving themselves as self-reliant is exceedingly important for the positive self-image of older persons living in SRO hotels. In fact, self-reliance and fear of dependency emerge as the *sine-qua-non* of the older hotel population. In time of need, most residents report that they request help from "nobody," but try to handle problems themselves. When problems become unmanageable, utilitarian arrangements with internal caretakers and other residents or other strategies are relied upon.

"Dependency of crisis" is one of the few types of dependency allowable among hotel residents.[2] This is situational dependency arising from personal crises such as illness, accident, alcoholism, or unemployment. It is time limited. If illness goes beyond the appropriate time span, the afflicted person comes to be defined as a burden. With the opportunity for role reciprocity lacking, the person is defined as having nothing of value to provide to others in exchange for his care.

In one case, a hotel resident was assisting another resident who was too weak to obtain his own food. The helping pattern persisted for several months until other residents in the hotel began to criticize the helper because he was contributing to the man's dependence.

The care extended by hotel staff, neighbors, and others is not binding and is only semipersonal, thus minimizing the feelings of dependency that the old residents perceive. As discussed earlier, friendships are not based on mutually binding relationships between confidants as much as on noncommittal, instrumental, and utilitarian factors.

Maintenance of autonomy, freedom, and privacy means that mutually supportive relationships are long in forming. Some persons are able to establish such relationships. Most commonly this happens in situations where two people form a "helping pair." Since women are scarce in the hotels, and central to most helping pair relationships, there is only a minimal opportunity for long-term and stable helping arrangements to emerge.

Residents are interested in people only insofar as they do not limit or threaten their own freedom. Overall, members of the older SRO population reveal very little about themselves to others. Neighboring in each other's rooms, frequent use of the telephone, eating together, or traveling together is uncommon under normal circumstances. Visiting occurs only when persons are ill or in crisis, because the norm is for social interaction to take place in public areas (lobbies, hallways, elevators, restaurants, sidewalks). Furthermore, the pattern of independence and self-reliance coupled with the need for freedom manifests itself in the avoidance of community organizations and agencies.

There is only a small amount of money circulating in the hotel environment. A dominant rhythm in the SRO world is the flow of money into the community at the beginning of each month with the arrival of Social Security and various benefit checks. This money is quickly allocated for room rent and the necessities of life, such as food, medicine, and small entertainments, etc. Since most of the older residents are dependent on a fixed minimal income, there is little chance that reserves can accumulate. This factor furthers their real dependency on the low rent housing, cheap restaurants, and the formal and informal services available to them.

Although they are minimal payments, Social Security and other benefits are reliable. This fact locks the managers of hotels into a symbiotic relationship with older tenants. Through them, the hotels are assured an inflow of working capital each month. As reported earlier by the manager of the Ballentine, the permanents are the "bread and butter" of the hotel operation.

The fixed minimal incomes of most residents force them into a delicate economic balance with their surroundings. They are particularly vulnerable to economic fluctuations resulting from inflation, as well as efforts to upgrade or improve their quality of life. For example, older residents in the Ballentine view hotel improvements with ambivalence, since improvement may mean higher rent. As one older resident reported,

> If he paints the walls, he's going to wanna raise the rent. I'd rather see the paint peeling off the walls and the carpet in shreds than have him slap on another $5.00 or $10.00 a month. My room is neat and clean, so I just don't give a damn about the hallways. It's just an excuse to raise the rent.

While improvements are viewed with suspicion, basic maintenance of the hotels and basic services are expected. Thus, tenants at the Ballentine remain bitter because (they say) with every increase in rent, some services are cut out.

Organizationally, through the extension of credit and favored status, hotels offer a buffer to the exigencies of strict economic restraints. We have seen that in the context of the hotel and of the larger urban infrastructure, residents can make informal arrangements about overdue rent and, in some cases, rely on hotel staff or neighbors for loans. The tolerance within the setting allows for informal arrangements to assure that basic needs are met and that feelings of independence are preserved.

Foods

Inexpensive hotels are not the only feature of the urban environment that assist tenants in meeting basic needs on a minimal amount of money. Low priced restaurants provide another major support component for hotel residents.

Getting food is a biological necessity as well as a social

psychological phenomenon.[3] There are no cooking facilities or refrigerators in hotel rooms. In general, tenants must leave the hotel and eat at nearby restaurants. The area south of Broadway is sprinkled with over fifty restaurants. Some of them offer basic, but adequate, menus for very reasonable prices. Having access to downtown restaurants, older tenants are able to obtain an adequate diet and degree of social interaction.

The five restaurants most used by tenants of the Ballentine are located within a three-block walking distance. Three of the restaurants are operated by Chinese families and offer meals at amazingly low prices. The menus are strikingly similar in all three, offering a selection of beef, chicken, and fish dishes which include vegetables, rice, bread, and coffee for $1.00 to $1.50. One of the restaurants, the Jupiter, sells meal tickets. An individual buys a ticket for $5.00 or $10.00 and is entitled to a 10 percent discount on the already low priced meals. Each time the individual has a meal, the ticket is punched. Some tenants buy meal tickets at the beginning of each month when money is available. In this way, when their cash runs low at the end of the month, meals have already been bought.

A striking characteristic of the Chinese restaurants is the lack of social interaction between the operators and the patrons. As well, there is a noticeable lack of conversation among the customers. With such low prices, the restaurants depend on a high turnover of customers and do not encourage persons to just sit and talk. Their object is to get people in and out quickly.

Some of the older tenants of the Ballentine are reluctant to use one of the Chinese restaurants because it borders on the "black" area of the downtown.

In all five of the restaurants, there are large signs stating that "No Credit" will be extended. However, individuals who are steady customers, and known and liked by the owners, are extended credit in special circumstances.

One (non-Chinese) restaurant located around the corner from the Ballentine delivers meals to persons in the hotel. The delivery service is critical for several of the older tenants who are marginally ambulatory and in chronically poor health. In the case of one older paraplegic, meals are delivered each afternoon by the waitress on duty. The waitress is familiar with the man and receives a small tip (usually 35 cents) for delivery meals.

The Wells Fargo Grill is a popular restaurant for tenants of the Ballentine and other downtown hotels. In comparison to the Chinese restaurants, the "Grill" offers a larger selection of food at slightly higher prices. While continually busy, the "Grill" has a more conducive atmosphere for just sitting around, talking, and drinking coffee. There is a feeling that the manager and waitresses (mostly middle-aged women living in the downtown) go out of their way for the elderly patrons. Many of the waitresses and patrons know each other on a first name basis; friendly interactions are common.

Waitresses frequently express concern for elderly patrons, listen to their stories, joke with them, or scold them for not eating properly. In a similar fashion some of the older tenants regard certain waitresses as friends and consider their interactions with them a highlight of their day.

The daily rhythm of choosing a restaurant and going out to eat is perhaps the most obvious behavioral pattern for older residents. Many elderly tenants eat only two meals a day, one in the morning and the other in the mid to late afternoon. Choosing a restaurant is frequently dependent on what type of food they wish to eat. For example, one older man preferred the liver and onions at one restaurant and the pancakes at another.

Some of the tenants have poor eating habits and suffer from malnutrition. However, this appears to be a matter of carelessness and ignorance rather than inadequate funds. Those who eat poorly spend an amount comparable to those who eat well but spend it on "junk" food. The worst cases of malnutrition are found among those who drink too much. As their cash resources dwindle, buying wine or vodka takes priority over food.

Some older tenants have hot plates in their rooms for

heating soup, or water for instant coffee. A few persons have toaster ovens or refrigerators for storing milk, cold cuts, and other perishable items. Persons who prepare meals in their rooms on a regular basis must shop daily. Such a strategy is problematic for most older tenants since no reasonably priced grocery stores are convenient to the downtown.

Thus, the "cheap" restaurants south of Broadway provide accessible and affordable meals to older SRO tenants. Equally important are the psychological benefits derived from having a choice of where, when, and what to eat.

Inexpensive public transportation further enhances living in the downtown. The "Senior bus pass" allows persons sixty-five and over to ride the buses for an average cost of 10 cents/ride. One seventy-five year old man said,

> I can ride from Tijuana to La Jolla, over fifty miles, and it costs me pennies. That means I can get out and see things. I used to ride the Greyhound everywhere. That's cheap too. I always go out to the ocean, La Jolla, or Mission Beach.

Since most of the bus routes pass through the downtown, residents find themselves at the hub of local transportation.

Living in the downtown, with its hustle and bustle, places the older hotel resident in contact with a wide variety of people. This means that any park or bus bench can become a seat for "street theatre." Many older residents spend hours sitting on bus benches watching people go about their business, enjoying the sun, sometimes engaging in conversations. A common practice is for residents of the Ballentine and other hotels to go to the "Plaza," a public square with a small fountain and a few benches, palm trees, grassy areas, and a tourist information booth. The Plaza is located in the heart of the downtown and is the focal point for bus transit in San Diego. It is aswarm with people of all sorts, conditions, and ages. A typical scene is for older persons to be sitting on benches, preachers to be saving souls, young backpackers to be milling about, and alcoholics sitting or sleeping on the grassy areas.

"Getting By"

In comparison to the elderly poor living in SRO hotels in some other cities such as New York and Detroit, those living in San Diego are doing quite well. Although they suffer as much from meager economic resources, multiple mental and physical impairments, and lack of access to community services, they benefit from San Diego's climate, a relatively benign "tenderloin" area, and still inexpensive hotels and restaurants.

For example, San Diego's mild climate frees the older person from harsh winters necessitating warm clothing. Most older residents get by with meager wardrobes frequently purchased at local secondhand "thrift shops." In fact, many tenants report that they purposely dress in worn clothes to give the impression they have no money. This particular strategy wards off persons who might try to hustle or in some way exploit them.

As stated above, when asked how they are doing, most say that they are getting along pretty well in spite of their problems. This response, however, varies depending on the age of the respondent. Persons sixty-five and over tend to be more positive about their situation than younger people. Their incomes hover near $300—an amount which allows them to "make it" in the hotels without having to "hustle."[4] Thus, the postretirement group is less likely to engage in hustling than the younger cohort of preretirees. The preretirees are more likely to be on some form of public assistance averaging less than $200 a month—a sum inadequate for living in any environment. They live in the worst poverty and are forced to find ways to supplement their incomes through conventional and unconventional means.

In general, there are few employment opportunities for persons over fifty because of discriminatory employment practices. The cohort of fifty to sixty-five year olds living in hotels find themselves at the bottom of the barrel. They often lack marketable work skills and have a disproportionate level of physical and emotional problems. Many have chronic drinking problems and irregular and erratic work histories.

Irrespective of age, persons with drinking problems are most likely to be involved in unconventional strategies for earning extra money. It is they who most frequently mismanage their money and come up short toward the end of each month.

The few people who manage to secure conventional jobs must settle for low paying and unstable employment. Such jobs include part-time janitorial work, washing dishes, or selling newspapers. Several persons have established relationships with various shop owners and make extra money by watching the store or business when the owner steps out for a lunch break or runs an errand. One man opened and closed a laundromat located near the hotel every morning and evening. Another man had a small janitorial business. Early each morning, he would clean two small card rooms located in the neighborhood. In exchange for these services, they make a minimum wage. Salaries are commonly paid on an informal basis and are not reported as earned income. Most individuals engaged in regular part-time work are fearful of "officials" finding out about their jobs and taking steps to have their Social Security, disability, or welfare checks reduced.

One of the higher status jobs available to older hotel residents is that of hotel desk clerk. As discussed above, the low pay is offset by the relative power, authority, and favored status the job affords.

Older residents in the Ballentine are involved in several unconventional activities for obtaining money and other goods. In their order of importance these activities include: (1) "go-fors," (2) "conning" or "running a line," (3) scavenging, and (4) borrowing.

One of the most popular means for making extra money is to make "runs" or "go-fors." This activity necessitates that the "runner" cultivate one or several individuals who need assistance. Persons needing assistance may be ill, incapacitated, or simply too busy or lazy to obtain their own alcohol, cigarettes or food. In exchange for the "go-for," the "runner" is given a payment of approximately 25 cents. At the Ballentine, one older tenant was particularly successful at making money through "go-fors." On weekends when the bars were filled with military men on leave, he would go from one bar to the next taking orders for food or cigarettes. He would then go to a local fast-food restaurant, fill the orders, then make the delivery to his customers. On a good night, he was able to earn from $10 to $15.

The "con" or "running a line" is a hustle involving varying degrees of verbal deception. The person "running a line" presents a story (often involving hard luck)aimed at eliciting sympathy or some other desired emotional response. Typically, the person being conned is from outside the hotel or the environment and is in a vulnerable position. For example, shortly after I began living in a downtown hotel, I was conned by an older black hotel resident. The "line" (story) was built around the racial prejudice he had suffered and was aimed at eliciting guilt (and, most importantly, a cup of coffee). Over coffee he explained his uniqueness as a con artist—panhandler. "I'm not a common panhandler. I don't just ask for money or a loan. I give you something for your money—a conversation about myself, what I've experience or read. I mean people enjoy when I run a line on 'em." As noted by Stephens, the higher the degree of verbal skill, the better the "con job," and the more successful the individual will be in gaining the desired end.[5]

A form of the "con" frequently involving older residents is that of a younger hotel resident or maid who cultivates a relationship with an older tenant as a means to exploit financial or material resources. The con artist gains the trust of the older tenant and provides minimal services and affection for as long as the older person has the resources to buy them.

Scavenging is a hustle practiced by only a few of the older hotel residents. It ranges from a simple practice of checking the change returns in public telephone booths and vending machines to actively collecting items from public refuse bins. The latter practice is not common among tenants living in the Ballentine. Such behavior is viewed as demeaning and possibly appropriate for some "skid row character," but certainly not for a resident of the Ballentine.

Borrowing is a form of panhandling practiced by some older SRO tenants. Outright begging is seldom seen, but persons will "borrow" money or a cigarette with little intention of paying it back in full. Some will ask for a loan and repay it promptly, then come back and ask for an increased amount of money. The next payback will not be for the full amount borrowed, and the deficit between the amount borrowed and the amount paid back will increase until a confrontation ensues or the debtor moves.

Such forms of hustling as prostitution, pushing drugs, or shoplifting are not commonly seen among older SRO tenants. Their hustles are seldom illegal or intended to make any substantial sums of money. In most cases, they are intended as a means for structuring time and providing some amusement and social interaction.

Notes

1   Personal communication from Paul Bohannan, 1976.

2   M.F. Lowenthal, "Social Isolation and Mental Illness in Old Age," *American Sociological Review* 29, no. 1 (1964): 54-70.

3   H.S. Maas and J.A. Kuypers, in their *From Thirty to Seventy* (San Francisco: Jossey-Bass, 1974), a longitudinal study of aging, discovered that men of lower socioeconomic status tended to be "loners," leading home-based lives focused on leisure time activities. Their relationships with their wives were not close or expressive, and in general they were not sociable, even when members of the kinship network lived close by. See also, M.F. Lowenthal and B. Robinson, "Social Networks," in *Handbook of Aging and the Social Sciences*, ed. R.H. Binstock and E. Shanas (New York: Van Nostrand Reinhold Company, 1976), p. 438.

4   M. Clark and B.G. Anderson, *Culture and Aging* (Springfield: Charles C. Thomas, 1967), p. 380.

5   Lowenthal, "Social Isolation," 375.

9

Life Trajectory Patterns

The life histories of SRO hotel residents follow several identifiable trajectories or patterns. There are three broad patterns of life adjustment discernable among residents: (1) the lifelong loner; (2) the retreatist or marginally socially adjusted; (3) the late isolate.

The first two patterns conform to what Paul Bohannan has called a "retreat into anonymity." While the range of personality types in SRO hotels is wide, in terms of life adjustment, he states that,

> They have renounced not only intimacy (and with it family relations, intimate sexuality and even close friendships); they have also renounced many roles—particularly producer and worker (which cannot be explained by the fact that many are unskilled—many unskilled workers are deeply tied to work roles), active citizen, community member. This is a true "retreat into anonymity."[1]

"Lifelong loners" view themselves as such. They often report traumatic and disruptive childhoods which thrust them into early self-reliant behavior. The marginally adjusted develop a retreatist and "loner" life style in early or middle adulthood. Both behaviorally and demographically, hotel residents resemble the community isolates discussed by Lowenthal.[2] They are predominantly single men of low socioeconomic status. Many of the San Diego hotel residents are second and third generation Northern Europeans.

The Lifelong Loner

Older persons who "fit" the description of life-long loner adopted the pattern early in life, grew up having experienced the Great Depression and the economic instability that followed it. Geographic mobility was an important aspect of their lives and job histories. Many worked in mobile and seasonal occupations (longshoremen, loggers, itinerate laborers, resort staff); some others made the military a career.

While some of the group are extreme isolates and avoid even casual friendliness, others are gregarious. For example, one sixty-four-year-old man had remained single his entire life and took pride in his past career as a resort waiter. "I worked the 'circuit' at some of the most known and exclusive resorts in this country." He enjoyed his work because it had kept him in contact with the public and allowed him to live in beautiful areas of the U.S. His worsening health forced him into early retirement and his painful arthritis coupled with heart trouble caused him to "slow down." However, he felt positive about his present life. He was still functional and able to maintain his sense of autonomy. He could afford his own room in a small inexpensive hotel, enjoyed the San Diego weather, and spent a lot of time near the ocean. As he told me:

> ... I keep busy cleaning my room, doing my laundry, and traveling around town on the buses. Every so often I get together with some friends and we go to a show. I've learned to listen to myself and not overdo it. Yeh, things are pretty good.

Many of the lifelong loners consider themselves to have lived interesting and nonconformist lives. For most, loneliness is not a problem since they have had many years of practice at the life-style.

If they ever wished for a conventional life-style, they failed or voluntarily rejected it early on and from that point tracked differently.

The following case history of a sixty-eight-year-old SRO resident named Olin McFarland gives some feeling for the life trajectory of a lifelong loner.

I was born in a small Massachusetts town. My age is sixty-eight. I was raised in a town and went to school as far as the seventh grade.

Mother was generally home and my father worked. My mother took in laundry to supplement my father's income. Father worked in the textile mills. He was a good provider. He didn't make much money, but he did the best he could. We were poor and always lived in the cheapest quarters and ate the cheapest food.

My father used to drink a lot. In those days they used to punish you for anything you done. It was sort of severe—he'd get one of those big razor straps and beat us for anything he thought was wrong. I was a likely target.

Like all mothers, mine was very good. She was busy most of the time, but anything I wanted, naturally, even if it cost money, she did her best. I had two brothers; one died, and I had a sister. I didn't have too much interaction with them, and I never did because of the age difference, and they were much brighter. My sister was much brighter than I was. In school I was always left back. It hurt to be left behind.

As I told you, I left school at the seventh grade. I tried to stay in school, but I wasn't too good a student. Actually, I had an accident when I was five years old. I was badly scalded. That made me sort of shy and retiring. The scars aren't too noticeable, but it did affect me . . . not quite retarded, but it causes me not to be too smart. It slowed down my thinking.

I got along pretty well with my parents, but in the depression days things were very lean, so at about 16, I went to New York City and things were much better, and the climate was much warmer. I worked on and off in New York. I worked for WPA for a while. I went to Orange Mental Hospital and worked there for about six months. In the summertime I worked at resorts which lasted about two or three months and then came lean times. I would find odd jobs—labor type—two or three days a week. I made enough to get just a cheap room and three small meals.

I think the depression really had an effect on me. I mean it was rough, jobs... in them days soup and a little bit of meat was a big banquet. I was always scared starvation will be again.

During the depression I learned that I had to take care of myself. People had to help themselves, so couldn't be much help to you. I had to do it pretty much on my own.

The next thing I remember there was Pearl Harbor. They wanted recruits, so I volunteered—in 1942. They were hectic years in Pearl Harbor. During the war time there were a lot of war scares. Anytime an unidentified plane came over, it all turned to darkness—blackouts.

I remember the blackouts and the big invasions and they were taking over island after island. All around the entire island of Honolulu, there was barbwire because they were afraid they were going to invade. All the ships in Pearl Harbor were on the bottom. I liked Pearl Harbor very much. The lean days were over. Meals weren't the best but plentiful.

At first I was working every day, then finally got one day off a month. I was working ten hours and they cut it down to six days a week instead of seven.

Probably the best time in my life was right after the war. Things were good—steady job, steady paycheck, and I did save up some money. I stayed there after the war and things got back to normal. There was a small layoff, maybe two or three months. Then came Korea. Then they called everybody back to work.

I worked on three shifts—mostly electrician, checking up the substations and battery maintenance. They furnished a pick-up. I lived in Bachelor Quarters. Those married had different quarters.

I spent my free time at a bowling alley, and most of my friends were other bowlers or friendly rivals.

I must have spent fifteen years over there, but then I got sick. I got emphysema and I got a disability discharge. I moved back to El Cajon, California. Emphysema was my first illness. It came on pretty gradually. I believed it was caused from fumes from the battery acid.

When I moved to El Cajon, I tried to start a business, but it was a failure. It lasted about six or seven months. I opened up a coin shop as I had some coins, but a burglary just about ruined that. That coin shop lasted less than a year, then I opened up another coin shop around the corner. A hold-up ruined that. Even though they got the man, they didn't recover the money. The man went to prison. Then I worked off and on in a parcel wrapping service and that was only seasonal. The rest of the time I couldn't even make expenses.

Now that I'm older, things are better. That might be the best thing about being old. You always have social security and you do have a pension, and you know you are not going to starve or no depression, or at least none in my life. Security is the main thing.

I've lived in the hotel for some years now. I like it, but the only thing is that the rents keep going higher and higher. Just this month they raise it another $15. That's a staggering blow to anyone on a fixed or limited income. That $15 means a lot. The service is not so good. The help is independent. They can get another job anyplace.

Anyway, I still have enough money that I can go down to the racetrack on Saturday. During the week I go down to the stockbrokers and watch the stock market quotations over the big board. I fiddle with stocks in a very small scale. Like everything else, you learn by trial and error. My first investments were not too good, but they are getting better because they couldn't get any worse.

I don't have friends in the hotel. Generally the friends I have are concerned with the stock market or horse playing. We talk about our common interests. I'll see people I know at Caliente (the racetrack in Tijuana, Mexico) on Saturday. I take the bus down just about every Saturday. You know, in the beginning I used to do pretty well on the horses, but the more you know about it the less chance you have of winning cuz you can't beat the horses in the long run. Nobody can. The challenge is there, and you keep on trying.

I've always been alone. I've had a few girlfriends off and on. Naturally, I don't have too good a personality. It seems I always disagreed with them. They wanted me to dress up in the height of fashion, and I wouldn't. That was one of the big drawbacks. Another one was I didn't know how to dance and

> they did. Oh yes, one leg is a little shorter than the other, and I think the girls noticed that too.
>
> I've never been married—that's a big responsibility. In younger days I didn't have it too good so it's a big responsibility and liability. If you have money, you generally get honey; no money, no honey.

Olin McFarland is a quiet and nice man. People in the Ballentine like him but know little about him. He gets along reasonably well and is functionally healthy. His work is built around his activities of horse racing and watching the stock market fluctuations. He is slightly better off financially than some other hotel residents. The stability that his $350 pension affords is exceedingly important for him emotionally. He views himself as old, but states, "I try to make the best of it even though I know that there isn't too much time left after the age of sixty-eight."

While he knows that his life could have been lived differently, he has integrated his past and perceived limitations into a coherent life story. From his perspective, he is able to explain why his life trajectory took its unique course.

The Marginally Social Adjusted

Those who sought a conventional life-style and failed made less favorable adjustments to hotel life than the lifelong loners. It was common for members of this group to be either self-recriminating or hostile, blaming failure on external situations. In either case, persons adjusting in this way had made marginal social adjustment all or most of their lives. For some, drinking problems and alcoholism had cost them "everything" and many reported past losses or hurts involving others. Marriages ended in divorce and many still regretted their earlier behavior. The following excerpt from my field notes reflects the defeatist pattern often resulting from alcoholism and injury.

> Lew stated that he has "learned to live with loneliness." He was once married, but his wife divorced him as a result of his

alcoholism. He has been sober since coming to San Diego in 1960. Previous to that he had been working in various jobs including truck driver, post office clerk, and payroll clerk. In 1946 he became a "Knight of the Road" or hobo, "... after the war there were no jobs, so I just took off." He spent time in every U.S. skid row. In 1960 he stopped drinking as a result of a San Diego judge threatening to send him to "camp" for one year. Says his police record is "two feet long." In 1958 he was injured in a truck accident and has not worked steady since that time.... He is struggling to get an increase in his Social Security (he receives $257/month). With inflation he has had to give up short trips. This contributes to his "spells of depression." About his family he said, "Well, my family was very close-knit and strict. Jesus, were they strict. We never had much company. My mother was a nervous person.... I think my father made her that way." He mentioned that he was very shy with women, "I haven't been with a woman since my divorce in 1958."

Some of the most hostile persons had spent time in prison (the "joint") and blamed "the system" for many of their problems. Their prison experience had locked them into a life trajectory of marginal social adjustment.

The following life history is illustrative of a person who had made marginal social adjustments throughout his life. Although he tried a conventional life-style of marriage and family, it ended in divorce. While married, he had little expressive or close ties with his wife and family. Now, in old age, contact with his children is almost nonexistent.[3] He attempted to be different, yet failed, leading the life of a "loner." Past and present problems with drinking have complicated and contributed to his difficulties in living.

My name is Joe Nabchuk and I'm sixty-six. I was born in Czechoslovakia and came to the U.S. when I was three years old with my father, mother, and older brother. I have four brothers and four sisters, and to tell the truth, I don't remember all the ages, but I'm the second oldest.

Well, my mother was a grand person.

When I was about twelve, my father (he was working in the steel mills) would grab my mother by the hair, which went

down to her hips, and throw her around. Even as young as I
was, I'd grab him and knock him down. I was a strapping
tough kid—raised in a tough neighborhood. He cut that stuff
out.

My mother was, in my opinion, a beautiful woman. When she
was in Europe, swimming in a pool, someone threw a rock and
put one of her eyes out. She was one eyed since she was about
12 or 13. I tried to buy her an artificial eye, but she didn't
want it. The one eye was just closed up all the time. She was
not only beautiful, everybody thinks their mother is beautiful,
but she was the most understanding person in the world. She
gave us kids close attention—like we were kittens.

My father was a brute, just like I am. Oh, I am not a brute now,
because I have had a stroke, but I can fight yet. My father was
the most brutal person that you would come in contact with.
He had to have his way or else you suffered for it.

We were poor. My father worked in the mills some of the
time. Other times he would go down to the railroads and get
old R.R. ties and cut them up for firewood. My mother would
make clothes out of flour bags and make the clothes fit the
next youngest when they were too small for the older kids.

My mother and father used to take in boarders. I made the
moonshine. They would keep me out of school to do it. That is
why I don't have much education. I started to drink at six to
seven years of age. I used to crawl under the table—there
would be ten to twelve people at it—and pour what was left
in the bottom of everybody's jug together and drink it. I
would drink quite a bit, but it didn't affect me. Once I went to
school and one of the teachers smelled it on me and she beat
me on the calf, so I broke away from her and went home. I am
trying to show you how ignorant things were. I went home
crying like I was killed. My dad asked what was wrong. I told
him and he grabs me, drags me down to the school and raised
hell saying, "Nobody beats my kid except me." They called
the police, he got arrested. Then my uncle got him out for
$10, he came home and beat the living shit out of me.

There was one instance with the school principal. I played so
much truancy that it was pathetic. She came up to me and
said, "We are going to have to do something about you." She
gave me the responsibility of picking up the money the kids
were saving from *all* the classes and taking it to the bank.

There was some money missing, and the others blamed me. The principal stuck up for me. They found out it wasn't me. I will never forget her as long as I live.

I never had much contact with the roomers. I'm not trying to make myself sound so old, but in my time, children were to be seen but not heard. Even my relatives, like my uncle, had nothing to do with kids at that time.

I left home at about twelve or thirteen, and I've never had much contact with any of my brothers or sisters since then. Like we never had much of a family life anyway. Everybody was trying to outdo the other one. They were going to be politicians, like my older brother Dick. He was running for councilman, and when he lost, he blamed me because I had gone to the penitentiary.

When I left home, I just grabbed a freight train. Wherever the train went, I went. I did that for about ten years. I remember that people were generous. I could always get something to eat. Today, it's dog eat dog. You can get a drink a lot quicker than you can get a baloney sandwich.

I've been a house painter all my life. My first job was as a painter back in northern Ohio. I am a painter and a good one—a professional. I am not bragging. I worked for myself as a painting contractor and a large painting company here in San Diego. A painter is a boomer. They work for two weeks, six months, or one year. Then they take off for where the grass is greener. They talk about all the people out of work. Fifty percent don't want to work and the other 50 percent don't have any skills. The longest time I ever stayed with one company was seven to eight years, a couple of different times. I've done a lot of other work too, like concrete work, carpentry, and laborer, but any time I did a paint job, that was my pride and joy. I would stand back on the scaffold and say, "Look at the beautiful job I did."

Then in 1930 I was in jail for five years. I was in for armed robbery. It was my first attempt at it, and it taught me a good lesson. I'll never take anything that isn't legal. I can make more panhandling and eating at the Mission than robbing a place, then spend five years paying for it. In prison, if you don't fit in, you had a *rough, rough* time. I fit in because I was bad mean. I took after my old man. I weighed 230 pounds. I could whip my weight in wild cats, like my old man, but that didn't mean anything if you didn't fit in. You had to fit into one of the groups way of thinking, or it became even rougher.

It wasn't drink that caused the robbery. It was a case of trying to get a large sum of money at one time.

Oh yeh, I was married at the time of that robbery. It was about 1928. I met her at the Moose Club in Montana. She ran a beauty parlor. We had two kids—a boy and girl. Christ, they must be near forty-five years old now. I have four grandchildren in upstate New York. I see them about every five years, but there is no close contact. I guess that's due to the experiences I've had with my brothers and sisters. I don't get too close with anybody. They thought they were better than the others—each and every one. I thought they would progress farther, which never happened. They never amounted to a hill of beans, so I don't know what they gained by it.

My wife divorced me while I was doing my time. We never had too much hopes and dreams.

We spent a lot of time with each other over a cup of coffee and a cigarette before I would go off to work. I went to work and would go to the bar after to about six or seven, then go home to eat. She would want to know where I was and I would say, "What do you care." She would say, "Your dinner is cold." I would say, "Serve it anyway." Then I would have a fifth of whisky and some beer, knock myself out, go to bed, get up in the morning, go to work.

When I got out of jail, I was on parole. I had no wife so I just worked around as a painter. I've told you all that. I haven't done anything outstanding in my life. My concerns have been to be healthy.

When I was younger and in a position to do things, my job and a home for my wife was important. I never thought much about it. I just took it day by day. I went to work every day, brought my check home every week and there was no future, because I had no education, no background, no connection, so what could I have planned for the future.

The biggest plan I got now is to be getting ready for the undertaker. I'll do that by just living day by day and when my time comes, I have to go.

So what about now. I'm old, and it's a small minority that is still active. I am except for my legs. I am getting tired of talking about my legs. I have talked about them three times. The average man, sixty to seventy years old, are good. I know lot of them, but then you find some who are grumpy, crabby, and feel they have been wompt]beat° on and somebody owes them a living.

Social Security gives you a steady income. If you have a steady income, life is pleasant.

I like people like me. I will give you an example: Since I lived in San Diego for about twenty years, I know everybody and in the hotels where I lived everybody comes to sit next to me even if there are sixteen other chairs vacant. They will come to me, speak to me all the time and borrow money from me when I have got it. So, how in the hell can they feel about me, unless they are using me, and I don't give out that much money.

My concerns are to rest my weary bones at night, get up in the morning, have a drink, and enjoy myself and let the rest of the world go by. I can't do anything about it. It hasn't done anything for me other than let me live. It gets tough to live. The prices, the way they are, plus they fucked up my check and I don't even know where I will sleep tonight and the only money I got is what you are going to give me. I used to be able to sleep under stairs and in boxcars, when I was broke, but I am getting too old and my legs are too stiff to keep that up. I smoke, but have to roll my own to be able to afford that.

I have lived in every flop house in San Diego except the El Toro, and I think they should leave these hotels. If you have to go to the Saint John]a retirement hotel°, you have to dress up to eat anything and they try to run your life for you. I have been drinking all my life, and I have conducted myself in a good manner, but if I had to live in a place like that, they would be on my ass all the time. In these hotels, as long as you pay, they don't care what you do as long as you don't kill anyone or burn the place down.

I keep on the move. People move in and out to look you over—who has the money, then they jack roll you. I got rolled just last week. I went to the liquor store and broke a $20 and put $18 in my pocket. I had more money on me, but I don't keep it in my pocket. I was ready to open the door to my hotel when two blacks grabbed me. They had me spotted because they knew which pocket to go into. They didn't take my billfold. Of course, I don't keep any money in that anyway. They threw me up against the glass door and it broke the glass all over the place. I didn't get hurt; my head is tough, just like my old man's.

The Late Isolate

Sprinkled among the vast majority of "loners" are few late isolates. For them, isolation has developed late in life, often since retirement. Members of this group can be classified as the old-old (seventy-five plus). They do not fit the pattern of lifelong isolation or marginal social adjustment, but instead have outlived their friends and family. They tend to live in the better SRO hotels which are moderately priced. More women belong to this group.

One late isolate, Mr. Biggs, has lived in the Ballentine for approximately eight months. Before moving into the hotel he and his wife lived in a small apartment. One year ago, she was put into a nursing home. Mr. Biggs had been caring for her, but found it increasingly difficult and was "forced" by the welfare department to "give her up."

After she left, he stated that he was "beside himself and terribly lonely." Someone suggested a hotel, so he put his furniture in storage and moved downtown. Mr. Biggs limits his interactions with other residents, stating that other tenants "can't talk about anything intelligent." Besides, he believes they are below him in status.

His present life is built around making daily visits to his wife in the nursing home. He believes that the care she receives is inadequate. He continually complains to various authorities that the home is a "rip off" and is not giving people the care they deserve for the money they pay. His complaints fall on deaf ears. One social worker who knows the case refers to him as a "senile old man."

In the time I knew Mr. Biggs, his health steadily deteriorated. He began to drink heavily. In conversations with him he could never reconcile the incongruity between his past life as a husband and provider and the present aloneness of a hotel. He never adjusted to his wife's illness and his change in life-style. He became increasingly aggressive toward people in the nursing home and hotel. Within a year he was forced into the hospital, then into an "extended care" facility.

For Mr. Biggs, the natural consequences of aging, i.e., the loss of spouse and others, proved devastating. He was unable, for whatever mental or physical health reasons, to replace lost relationships through a variety of substitutes. For him and others who have had a wife as lifelong confidant, living alone in a hotel is perceived as threatening, and adjustments are tenuous.

Most older people living in SRO hotels are disengaged from close interpersonal relationships, family, and community. However, for most residents, disengagement is not a result of the aging process, but instead a mode of adjustment possible at any point in the life cycle. As we have seen, for most persons living in the SRO hotel, aloneness has been a central focus of their style of coping with the world. Thus each individual must be considered in the context of his own life span development, unique circumstances and experiences, and slice of social history.

For most older SRO residents (regardless of the life trajectory pattern) there is a long ingrained impulse toward autonomy and self-reliance. Among the present older generation of men in our culture and especially the predominantly male culture of the SRO, the ability to keep on managing for onself, to make it alone, to reaffirm that one is still self-governing is of the utmost importance.

Denial of need, physical impairment, and social interaction are endured by many aging SRO residents so as to maintain independence and avoid the spectre of institutionalization. As Clark and Anderson [4] suggest,

> What in one case might seem to be a dangerous withdrawal from all social intercourse into a hermitage might, in fact, be a valid attempt to preserve self-esteem in the face of

acknowledged decrements in physical and mental functioning. If such decrements are not yet so severe as to merit professional or institutional care, we are obliged to acknowledge such withdrawal as reasonably functional to the individual's culturally-sanctioned need for autonomy and self-reliance.

An important aspect of older hotel residents' satisfaction and acceptance of hotel life is whether or not the "alone" pattern of living has been voluntarily chosen. For example, many late isolates feel forced into the hotels for health and financial reasons. If the change in circumstances are too drastic, poor adjustment and severe isolation may be the result.

In the case of "lifelong loners" the "alone" pattern of living is a voluntarily chosen alternative within the limits of perceived alternatives. For this group, the hotels are a natural habitat. The social climate of the hotels is well suited to their values, needs, interests, and finances. Lowenthal's assessment of this group is apropos,

> They liked being alone, and ... rarely mentioned loneliness as a problem of their past or current lives.... While such an alienated lifestyle might in itself be culturally defined as a form of mental illness, lack of interpersonal relationships, which is one of its main characteristics, may help [in old age] to prevent the development of overt psychogenic disorder.[5]

As long as their autonomy is not threatened through severe physical and mental decrement, the hotels provide an optimal living environment.

Those whose life followed a pattern of marginal social adjustment frequently blame the "system" or "others" for their present situation. Although the hotels and the commercial environment meet most of their needs, they feel unhappy, angry, or defeated about their situation. Rather than adjusting to problems associated with living and growing old, they seek escape via alcohol and isolation induced through mistrust and suspicion of others.

However unhappy with their life or present situation, older residents view the hotel as infinitely better than what lies beyond, i.e., some form of institutionalization. Hospitals and nursing homes are feared and are, they say, to be avoided at almost any cost. Institutions represent the "end of the line"; they are places for persons who have "given up" and can no longer live independent lives.

An eighty-one-year-old hotel resident sums up his experiences with hospitals and "rest homes" and his preference for the hotel.

> I said, "Well, I'm getting the hell out of this place [county hospital]." Next day I was on my way downtown. I come right down to this hotel and got a room. I come in without a wheelchair. I left the wheelchair on the sidewalk. Then when I came back Monday, well, with, of course, the wheelchair, the clerk said, "What's that?" "Oh," I said, "I use that once a great while." "Jesus Christ, you know we don't have wheelchairs in here." I says, "Too late now, I paid my room rent." So I went upstairs without my wheelchair, and I got by without it. A guy borrowed that wheelchair and he hocked it for $25 so he could play the horses. We'd go down and lay twenty-five dollars on a horse. I think he hocked it three times. He finally sold it. The guy still owes me forty bucks.

> I tried a resthome later on. I was in, what's the name of it? That's the last one I was in. I had to go out there or something. They didn't do me any good. They just . . . they're all the same. Just got your checks and that was it.

> I get up in the morning between ten and eleven. Same story every day. Sit around. Breakfast, not till ten or eleven o'clock. And I either get hotcakes, or two donuts and coffee or, short stack of pancakes, whatever you call them. Then, I have a decent supper at night time. Take no vitamins, no medicine . . . .

> Soon as I get up, I start to cough. And when I go to bed at night I have quite a time when I get into bed—getting a breath. I really puff and blow for ten or fifteen minutes. And all at once, I calm down. Some day I'm not going to calm down. I'm just gonna come up and choke me to death, I suppose.

> Just feel as good as anybody . . . as good as ever I did. But . . . my legs . . . I notice my legs from here down are almost

pink, like a lack of circulation or something. There's no blood ... Well, there's blood there, but it isn't circulating right.

No more resthomes. I'm better off here in the hotel. See, I can come and go anywhere, there ....

I couldn't do any better than right here. Everything is handy. If I could just get some strength in my legs. Course, I know I don't try to help myself, and that doesn't help me any either. I haven't been eating right for a long time. In fact, I never did. Never did have good meals, as you would say. Just any old thing is alright. I get by. I could afford to eat much better than I do but for some reason, I just don't do it.

Notes

1   F.L.K. Hsu, "American Core Value and National Character," in *Psychological Anthropology,* new edition (Cambridge, Mass.: Schenkman Publishing Company, 1959), pp. 241-62.

2   M. Clark, "Cultural Values and Dependency in Later Life, " in *Aging and Modernization,* ed. D.O. Cowgill and L.D. Holmes (New York: Appleton-Century-Crofts, 1972), p. 267. This excellent article on the concept of dependency in old age and its relationship to varying cultural modes and values, and the meanings it has assumed in Western thought—particularly in America—provides a discussion of the uses of dependency and a comparative cultural discussion of the subject. Other sources on the meaning of dependency in America include: Robin Williams, *American Society: Sociological Interpretation,* 3rd ed. (New York: Alfred A. Knopf, 1970); Richard Kalish, "Of Children and Grandfathers: A Speculative Essay on Dependency," *The Gerontologist* 7, no. 1 (1967):65-69, 79; Talcott Parsons, *The Social System* (New York: Free Press of Glencoe, 1951), pp. 428-473; Francis L.K. Hsu, *Psychological Anthropology: Approaches to Culture and Personality* (Homewood, Illinois: Dorsey Press, 1961); Margaret Clark and Barbara Anderson, *Culture and Aging* (Springfield, Illinois: Charles C. Thomas, 1967).

3   For example, David Gutmann, "The Hunger of Old Men," *Trans-Action* 9 (1971): 55-66, suggests that food takes on an added importance as persons age, especially men.

4   Hotel residents define a hustle as an unconventional way of earning extra money to supplement their limited incomes. A hustle lacks stability and may involve some physical risk. In some cases, a hustle involves illegal or socially unacceptable behavior.

5   B.J. Stephens, *Loners, Losers, and Lovers: Elderly Tenants in a Slum Hotel* (Seattle: University of Washington Press, 1976), p. 62.

10
The Underlying Enemy: Deterioration of Health

Health is an exceedingly important matter and underlying enemy for the older SRO resident. Although hotels provide supportive services in terms of housekeeping, security, and informal arrangements, it is necessary that older residents be able to tend to most of their own needs. From a functional health viewpoint, they must have a capacity to cope with getting their own food and doing what they need to do to keep going.

In most hotels, instances can be found where the management or a neighbor will assist someone who can no longer care for his own needs. However, such efforts are time-limited and usually in response to an emergency situation. Sustained care such as that provided in a nursing home for the chronically ill or disabled is difficult to maintain in a hotel even though it serves as a setting where limited support can be obtained.

This chapter focuses on the self-perceived health status of older SRO residents and the manner in which they use and do not use help from the traditional medical care services and others. When considering the health status of the older SRO resident or any individual, it is important to view health as a process of person-environment interaction within an ecological context and not simply a utopian state characterized by the absence of disease.

As Rene Dubos so perceptively stated:

> The concept of perfect and positive health (through eradication of disease) is a utopian creation of the human mind. It cannot become reality because man will never be so perfectly adapted to his environment that his life will not involve struggle, failures, and sufferings. . . . The less pleasant reality is that in an ever changing world each period and each type of civilization will continue to have its burden of disease created by the unavoidable failures of adaptation to the new environment.[1]

Diseased persons should not be automatically categorized as "not healthy" since "there is a healthy way to live a disease."[2] Health and disease are present in all situations. Since the level of self-perceived illness among SRO residents is high, our focus should be on adaptive and dysadaptive ways to live a disease, disability, or one's life. Again, Dubos has emphasized the situational aspects of health:

> It is not possible to define health in the abstract. Its criteria differ with the environmental conditions and with the history of the social group. The criteria of health are conditioned even more by the aspirations and the values that govern individual lives. For this reason the words health and disease are meaningful only when defined in terms of a given physical and social environment.[3]

Health becomes meaningful when we focus on individual functioning in specific social and physical environments. So considered, notions about health transcend biological-reductionist statements and center attention on the complexities of behavioral, physical and social features of individuals in environments. Our task is to observe people in natural settings, the supports that they receive, and the subjective responses they make to phases or aspects of living. Responses include coping, rallying, and attempting to overcome physical or psychic limitations when realistic. By coping I mean instrumental behavior and problem-solving capacities of persons in meeting life demands and goals.[4] It involves the application of skills, techniques, and knowledge that a person has acquired. Thus, health behavior is a complex series of techniques whereby individuals deal with the realities of limits (Limits or variables emanate from various levels—physical, emotional, age related, socioeconomic, ethnic or social class related, etc.).

Health care needs and services were examined against the background characteristics of those living in the hotels, their age, income, and life histories. The data were obtained from the random sample of residents through the administration of two questionnaires (containing Cornell Medical Index; the Index of Incapacity; and open-ended questions).

Health Substudy Questionnaires

Early in my fieldwork, the issues of health status arose as a central theme. Thus, in March, 1976, midway through the participant observation phase of research, a health questionnaire was administered to a stratified random sample ($N=75$) of older hotel residents from twelve hotels. The interviews were administered by myself and three professional interviewers from WBSI. The interview schedule included the Cornell Medical Index (CMI) and other pertinent health related questions. (See Appendix A). Questions pertained to: (1) the length of residence in the downtown area and reasons for living in the area; (2) who would help in time of emergency; (3) respondent's actual use of health services and how it is financed; (4) sociodemographic information (age, sex, ethnicity, education, marital status, marital history); (5) the 195-question Cornell Medical Index—questions related to the self-assessment of bodily symptoms, past illnesses, family medical history, behavior, moods, and feelings. Respondents were read each question, then asked to answer "yes" or "no." Indecision in responding as well as volunteered information was noted by the interviewer.

The CMI is a well-known health questionnaire developed in the United States and found useful in numerous medical situations. Over the years, studies have demonstrated its value as an aid to clinical diagnoses and the collection of medical histories;[5] as a medical screening procedure;[6] as an epidemiological tool;[7] as a test instrument for measuring self-perceived psychological and medical characteristics of noninstitutionalized aging people.[8]

Interpretation of the CMI was conducted with caution; however, the results presented here are suggestive of the overall self-perceived health status of older hotel residents. No attempt was made to infer specific diseases in the population—such analysis would necessitate thorough medical examinations. Scoring the CMI is a rather simple procedure; the entire number of "yes" responses is determined for each subject. A serious disorder is suspected when more than twenty-five items are marked "yes." Each CMI was scanned to determine clustering of "yes" responses in one or two sections. This indicated that the respondent's medical problems were localized. If the "yes" responses were scattered throughout the CMI, this indicated that the medical problems were diffuse, usually involving a psychological disturbance. "Yes" responses on sections "M" through "R" are important in determining psychological disturbances. Emotional disturbances may also manifest themselves through numerous "yes" responses on the sections "A" through "L" referring to many organ systems. The following configurations point to medically significant emotional disturbances: (1) a syndrome of "yes" answers clinically suggestive of a psychological disturbance; (2) thirty or more "yes" responses on the entire CMI; (3) three or more questions not answered, answered both "yes" or "no," or with changes or remarks written in by the respondent. Of these, the significance of "yes" responses has the most importance.

Various investigators have pointed to the usefulness and problems associated with using the CMI in epidemiological research.[9] For example, Abramson found the CMI to yield scores which were useful indicators of the degree of general emotional disability among respondents.[10] The CMI has also been found to be a valid indicator of general overall health status. However, without a clearer definition of what constitutes global health, the validity of the CMI in this respect is difficult to test.

Beyond the use of the CMI as an indicator of health status, responses may be taken at their face value. As Abramson suggests, the CMI may be useful as a measure of the amount, types, and patterns of complaints in a population.[11] Data of this sort are useful in anthropological studies as well as in the planning and provision of health and medical care services.

Numerous researchers have discussed the problems of using the CMI in comparative and cross-cultural research.[12] On the basis of their comments, it would seem that the CMI is of little value in comparative studies of health status in widely divergent cultures. Using the CMI in comparisons of subgroups of a population sharing the same language and common general culture is also problematic. Subcultural differences influencing the perceptions and reporting of symptoms exacerbate efforts to compare scores.[13] Other variables found to be associated with differences in CMI scores and having cultural connotations include age,[14] education level,[15] and urban living.[16]

In this study the CMI was used primarily as a measure of overall self-perceptions of health and as a tool for exploring the patterns of self-perceived complaints of older hotel residents. Since the population was relatively homogeneous in terms of sex, education, ethnicity, and age, problems of comparison are minimized. Although the CMI was designed as a paper and pencil questionnaire, we found that verbal administration of the questionnaire by trained interviewers avoided problems of illiteracy and physical impairments affecting reading and writing.

In general, interviewers encountered few problems in administering the questionnaire. Questions are clear, simply stated, and comprehendible to the SRO population. What problems were encountered were in sections in which questions seemed repetitious. For example, respondents commented on questions requiring individual definition, such as, "Do you suffer badly from frequent severe headaches?", or "Have you ever had a severe operation?" Persons would ask, "What do you mean by serious?", or "I don't know what you mean by frequent?" In this study, such ambiguity was viewed positively since it required the respondent to volunteer his private opinion and definition. Thus, the questionnaire identifies attitudes toward illness and stress as much as it gets to the facts about them.

In contrast to self-perceptions of bodily and emotional problems and symptoms, respondents were asked about their actual functional ability. The "Index of Incapacity" was designed by Peter Townsend for investigating old people living at home.[17] Townsend was aware that "the presence of a particular disease does not necessarily indicate for any given person inhibition of activity which results from it."[18] His approach focuses on the consequences of disease and injury and the kinds of activities an old person would have to perform to live alone. The index used in this study is similar to the abbreviated version of the Townsend scale used by Shanas, et al. in their cross-national survey.[19]

The index requires an answer to six questions from the older person: (1) Can you go out-of-doors? (2) Can you walk up and down stairs? (3) Can you get about in the house? (4) Can you wash and bathe yourself? (5) Can you dress yourself and put on your shoes? (6) Can you cut your own toenails? A person is asked whether they can do each of these tasks without difficulty and without assistance, with some difficulty but still without the help of another person, and finally, with difficulty and only with the help of another person. As a functioning member of the community, a person of any age must be able to leave the house and interact to some degree with the surroundings. Walking out of doors, up and down stairs, and caring for personal needs are a necessity for continued life in the community. As noted by Shanas:

> The inability to perform any one of the six tasks in the index
> without assistance from another person is an incapacitating
> handicap to an old person. Being unable to cut one's own
> toenails and the resulting foot problems may be just as great a
> handicap to the elderly person's daily functioning as a sensory
> impairment or the symptoms of a chronic disease.[20]

The ability to perform a task without any restriction is
assigned a score of zero, the ability to perform a task only with
difficulty is assigned a score of one, and complete inability to
perform a task is assigned a score of two. The scores for the six
tasks are summed, producing a range of physical incapacity from
zero to twelve. A score of zero means that the respondent could
perform all of the six activities by himself. A score of one means
that five of the tasks could be performed without difficulty, but
one could not. A score of seven or more indicates a serious
degree of difficulty with several activities and dependence in at
least one of the six activities.

When used in sociomedical research, the CMI and
"Index of Incapacity" allow respondents to evaluate their own
health as they perceive it. While the interchangeability of self-
perceived health and objective medical assessment has been
challenged,[21] other research has shown self-assessment of
health important and valuable in research on human
development, particularly in the later years.[22] When viewing
health as a process, individuals' perceptions about their own
condition become foremost. As Maddox and Douglas suggest:

> The subjective belief that one is healthy or ill may be more
> important than actual medical status in predicting an
> individual's general emotional state and behavior.[23]

Maddox's fifteen year longitudinal study of aging and health has
shown: (1) there is a persistent, positive congruence of self and
physician's ratings of health; (2) when an incongruence does
occur, there is a tendency for the individual to overestimate,
rather than underestimate, his health; (3) a substantial stability
was found between self and physician's rating through time; (4)
self-ratings of health were found to be better predictors than
future physician's ratings of health.[24]

There is considerable evidence that self-assessment of health is not random, but persistently and positively related to objective evaluation of health. In light of the underutilization of health care facilities and great difficulty in obtaining objective health data from the older urban poor, self-rating of health provided the most feasible approach.

Sample Characteristics

The formal sample consisted of seventy-five persons aged fifty years and older randomly selected from twelve hotels. The hotels ranged from low to moderate rent and were selected on the basis of geographical location within the study boundaries and whether 50 percent or more of the residents were permanent (i.e., judged on the basis of living in the same hotel for six months or more). After the hotels were selected, the sample size within each hotel was determined (see Table 5). Selection of individuals to be interviewed was accomplished through interviewing the hotel managers to determine the room number of those permanent residents over fifty years old. A table of random numbers was used to select the room numbers for those to be interviewed. The interviews took an average of one hour to administer. The refusal rate was thirteen percent. People refused to be interviewed because they were suspicious or confused over our motive for wanting health information. Mistakenly, some persons thought we were checking up on their eligibility for disability benefits.

The sample of seventy-five persons fifty years old and over consisted of sixty-seven males and eight females. This finding is similar to other studies,[25] mirroring the overrepresentation of males in SRO hotels. The mean age for the group was sixty-two years, with a range of fifty to ninety-three years of age. On the average, women were slightly younger (fifty-seven years) than men (sixty-three years). The respondents had from three to sixteen years of education, with a mean of 9.5 for the total sample.

Table 5

Sample Size from Individual Hotels

SRO Hotels	N
King George	5
Wells Fargo	20
Ballentine	5
General Lee	5
Chase	4
Sandmore	5
Santee	7
Monroe	3
La Mer	4
La Salle	11
Venus	5
Lincoln	1
Total	75

Almost all of the respondents were living alone—8 percent or four persons were married and several of these respondents were living separately from their spouse. Approximately one-fifth (22 percent) of the respondents had never married.

Over two-thirds of the sample population were below the retirement age of sixty-five yet only 9 percent of the total sample were employed full time. High unemployment was not a surprise since many middle-aged men living in hotels reported physical and emotional problems. On the basis of the CMI and participant observation, those in the fifty to sixty-four year age cohort appeared in worse shape (physically, emotionally, and financially) than those in older age categories. The large majority of respondents had job histories in manual (skilled or unskilled) or clerical occupations (94 percent).

The average total monthly income for respondents was $301. There was a tendency for those over sixty-five years of age to have a higher average monthly income ($321) than those under sixty-five ($286). A small number (10 percent) received income from wages; even fewer (4 percent) were receiving welfare payments. The majority of respondents (86 percent) received income from social security, SSI, pensions, disability, or veterans benefits.

The average and median length of time lived in the downtown was 7.8 and 5 years respectively. Seven of the respondents had lived in the downtown for more than twenty years. Approximately half of the respondents had lived in their present hotel from one to five years, one-third had moved there within the year, and the remainder (22 percent) had lived in the same hotel for more than six years. Table 6 summarizes the socioeconomic and residency patterns of the sample.

In summary, and as expected, the sample population had an overrepresentation of men living at the lower socio-economic level, yet maintaining themselves independently rather than through welfare funding. The population had lived in the downtown for some time and seemed to prefer the downtown hotel environment. When asked why they did not live north of Broadway, over half said that it was too expensive. One-third felt comfortable in the area and thought it was convenient to restaurants and stores.

Helping and Health Care Utilization Patterns

Several questions in the interview questionnaire concerned help-seeking patterns and the actual use of health services. Supporting independence and self-reliance as primary values among hotel residents, over one-half (57 percent) of the respondents would talk to "no one" about an illness before seeking professional medical care. Approximately one-tenth (13 percent) said they would consult a relative and 12 percent would seek help from a friend either inside or outside the hotel. Only 3 percent said they would discuss the matter with the

Table 6

**Socioeconomic and Residence Characteristics
of the Hotel Sample (*N*=75)**

	N	%
Sex		
Male	67	89
Female	8	11
Marital Status		
Married	2	5
Single/Never married	17	22
Divorced	33	43
Separated	10	13
Widowed	13	17
Age		
50-59	31	41
60-69	26	35
70-79	15	20
80-89	2	3
90+	1	1
Median = 61 years		
Mean = 62 years		
Education		
Elementary School	35	47
High School	24	32
College or More	16	21
Median = 9		
Mean = 9.5		
Types of Past Employment		
High Executive/major professional	—	—
Business Manager/lesser prof.	—	—
Administrative Personnel/		
minor prof.	5	7
Clerical/sales worker	9	12
Skilled manual	21	28
Semiskilled	19	25
Unskilled	21	28
Never worked	—	—
Currently Employed		
Yes	13	17
No	62	83
Residency in Hotels		
Less than one year	24	32
1-5 years	34	45
6-10	12	16
11-15	3	4
16-20	2	3
21-25	—	—
no response	—	—
Residency in Downtown San Diego		
Median 5 years		
Mean 7.8 years		
Monthly Income		
Median $289		
Mean $301		

hotel manager or desk clerk.[25] However, we know that some of those who said they would talk to "no one" did contact the manager or desk clerk if they needed emergency assistance. One seventy-one-year-old man reported, "I can depend on them. If I can get to my phone, they're up here in two seconds flat."

The first utilized sources of primary health care for the respondents were equally distributed between the private physician (32 percent) and hospital outpatient department (31 percent). Other health facilities utilized were hospital emergency rooms (15 percent) and the Veterans Hospital located in La Jolla (15 percent), sixteen miles north of the downtown. Only one SRO hotel resident mentioned using a Free Clinic for senior citizens located close to the downtown area.

MediCal and Medicare figure prominently in the financing of medical care among respondents. Thirty-eight percent of the respondents said that Medicare covered their hospital expenses; another 46 percent indicated that their hospital bills were covered by MediCal. Primary care expenses were paid by Medicare for 41 percent of the respondents and MediCal for 49 percent. There is some overlap in these two categories with respondents citing both as a source of medical coverage. Veterans benefits cover the medical expenses (hospital and primary care) for approximately 17 percent of the respondents. Other insurance or Workman's Compensation accounts for only 12 percent (hospital and primary care) of medical expense coverage, while 12 percent paid for hospital and 13 percent for primary care through personal finances. Some respondents were not able to tell us how their medical care was financed. It may be that relatives or conservators handle the financial affairs of some respondents. Some simply had not used a physician in the recent past. It is also suggested that many respondents are quite confused as a result of the "red tape" associated with medical expenses—thus the lack of response.

Confusion about Social Security, Veterans benefits, Medicare, and MediCal benefits was encountered in several instances. This confusion was often coupled with mistrust of bureaucratic state and federal programs. Initially, several respondents were distrustful of me, thinking that I was some type of investigator searching for ways to decrease the small amount of money they were already receiving.

Self-Reported Health Status Among Hotel Residents

Overall, self-perceived physical and emotional complaints were high. On the basis of self-perceived symptoms, serious physical disorders were reported by 69 percent of the respondents; emotional disturbances in 63 percent. Of the 63 percent of persons reporting emotional disturbances, all had serious physical disorders. These results indicated a strong correspondence between physical and emotional health among hotel residents as measured through the CMI (see Table 7).

A persistent health-related finding was the tendency for persons in the sixty-five to seventy year age cohort to have a more positive perception of health than those younger cohorts fifty to sixty-four years of age or those cohorts over seventy years of age (see Table 8). That those between sixty-five to seventy years of age reported fewer symptoms than those of the younger cohorts supports the findings of several studies.[27] In general, the findings suggest that for some individuals the self-assessment of health tends to improve after retirement. For those just over retirement age, a new degree of stability emerged with the freedom from sporadic and unsatisfying work and the provision of stable (though minimal) income through Social Security. Persons in the fifty to sixty-four year age cohort lived in some of the worst SRO hotels. They tended to be unemployed and prematurely excluded from the work force. Many were not able to find work as a result of their physical and emotional problems.

Nearly one quarter (23 percent) of the respondents felt they were always in poor health and frequently ill. About half of this group ($N=8$) were confined to bed with illness. Those reporting poor health tended to be living in the more

Table 7

Number and Percentage of Persons with Physical Disorders and Emotional Disturbances According to CMI Downtown San Diego Hotel Residents (N=75)

	Serious Physical Disorders		Emotional Disturbances	
	N	%	N	%
Indicated	52	69	47	63
Not Indicated	23	31	28	37

Table 8

**Analysis of Variance
for Scores
on the CMI by Age (N=75)**

Age Cohort	N	X Score°	Standard Deviation
50-55	20	42.9	24.8
56-64	28	46.6	26.7
65-70	11	26.6	16.1
71+	16	32.9	17.0

° Serious disorders are suspected when a person answers more than 25 questions positively, i.e., scores over 25, on the CMI. Persons in the 65-70 age cohort are the only group in which the mean score approaches the normal scoring level.

F ratio = 2.6, 3 df, p   .05

deteriorated SRO hotels and were below sixty-five years of age. This same group worried about their health and reported continual feelings of unhappiness. In many respects, the members of the younger cohort fit the category of the marginally socially adjusted discussed in the previous chapter. A portion were so pessimistic as to say they wished they were dead and away from it all. Nervous exhaustion, a symptom of depression, was reported by 20 percent of the sample—twelve of the fifteen making this complaint were below age sixty-five.

Chronic complaints were reported by 40 percent of the respondents. About one-third (32 percent) had been diagnosed by a doctor as having heart trouble. A greater proportion reported that they had been diagnosed as having blood pressure either too high (45 percent) or too low (19 percent). Approximately two-fifths (37 percent) reported that they had pains in the heart or chest. Again, cardiovascular complaints were more prevalent among those below sixty-five years of age and living in the more deteriorated SRO hotels. Those under sixty-five were twice as likely to report cardiovascular complaints as those over. Over one-fourth (28 percent) said they were crippled by severe rheumatism (arthritis). Approximately one-fourth (24 percent) had received medical treatment for tumor or cancer.

The common ailments usually associated with aging were readily evident in this population. A full 90 percent needed glasses to read and over one-third reported hearing difficulties. Complaints about eyes and ears were not significantly related to residence pattern or age.

Respondents were asked several questions about habits. Approximately two-fifths (39 percent) reported having great difficulty in falling asleep and staying asleep. Again, such problems were not related to residence or age. Over one third (37 percent) of the residents smoked more than twenty cigarettes per day. The excessive use of coffee and tea (more than six cups per day) was seen in 24 percent of the respondents. Of the twenty-eight persons who said they drank more than two alcoholic drinks per day, all were under sixty-five years of age.

Those over sixty-five who were alcoholics had learned to control their problem. Some attributed their survival into "old age" as a result of their change in behavior.

Musculoskeletal complaints, including stiffness in joints, painful legs, arms, back, and feet were most evident in the fifty to sixty-four year age cohort. The sixty-five to seventy-nine year age cohort reported fewer complaints in this area. Those over eighty showed a level of complaints comparable to the preretirement cohort. The latter groups' complaints probably reflect a genuine age-related effect. Disability and deformity were significantly related to being a member of the fifty to sixty-four year age cohort (p < .01). Questions about the nervous system included the frequency of headaches, dizziness, hot and cold spells, paralysis of body parts, nail biting and stuttering. The preretirement age group showed twice as many nervous system complaints as those over sixty-five. A portion of the respondents from SRO hotels had been patients in mental hospitals (14 percent). They were all persons in the fifty to sixty-five year old cohort. The relatively high number of ex-mental hospital patients probably reflects California's decision to close several state mental hospitals and return patients to the community. One-fourth (25 percent) felt they were extremely sensitive or shy. A similar percentage felt they had to be on guard even with friends.

Digestive system complaints were frequently mentioned by all the respondents. Four-fifths (81 percent) of them had lost more than half their teeth. Most of these persons did not have dentures. Visits to the dentist were infrequent across the sample. Stomach ulcers had been a problem for 15 percent of the respondents and 12 percent reported they had constant stomach troubles. About one-fifth reported that their appetite was always poor. One-third (33 percent) of the respondents felt that they were overweight, while 16 percent felt that they were underweight.

Several other complaints were reported by those interviewed. One-third of the residents reported serious injuries in the past. One-third (33 percent) reported that they had had venereal disease in the past. Serious operations in the past were reported by one-third of the residents. Approximately one-fourth (24 percent) complained about liver or gall bladder problems.

Tables 9 and 10 compare the score of the hotel residents on the CMI with other samples of adults living in various contexts. The level of perceived illness among older hotel residents is vividly illustrated when scores are compared to ostensibly "normal" sample populations and various types of hospital populations. The scoring profile of hotel residents approximates the profile of hospital patients with diagnosed emotional disturbances, rather than "regular" or "normal" populations. This finding underlines the physical and emotional "vulnerability" of the SRO hotel population.

Table 9

Proportion of Subjects Giving the Specified Number of "Yes" Responses on the CMI, for Five Samples of Men Compared to Male Hotel Residents

No. of "Yes" Responses	152 NY Hosp. Employee "Normals"	282 NY City Ostensibly Healthy	2,107 NY Hospital Patients	183 NY Hosp. Neurotic Patients	371 VA Psychiatric Patients	67 San Diego Hotel Residents
10 or more	28%	67%	71%	89%	97%	94%
20 " "	05	37	42	68	90	81
30*" "	03	10	23	52	76	52
40 " "	01	05	13	34	59	43
50*" "	01	02	08	26	45	31
60 " "	01	01	03	16	30	17.5
70 " "	00	00	02	08	20	9

The table reads, for example, at the scoring level of 50: 1% of the New York Hospital "normals," 2% of the New York City ostensibly healthy population, 8% of the New York Hospital patients, 26% of the New York Hospital neurotic patients, and 45% of the V.A. psychiatric patients gave 50 or more "Yes" answers.

*Suggested critical scoring levels.

Health Related Problems of Older Hotel Residents

Six months after the primary interview, another interview was administered to members of the original sample. Over half (*N*=41) of those originally interviewed were available for the functional health status survey. In the six months between the two interviews, twenty-three of the initial respondents had moved, three were in the hospital or too sick, and eight refused to be interviewed. The second interview asked questions about problems with present living situation and functional health capacity. When asked about chief problems in their life, health ranked first as an item of concern (54 percent). As a chief problem, poor health was not related to age or residential location. Chronic complaints such as arthritis, emphysema, and heart trouble were the most frequently volunteered complaints. Those in the seventy-one-plus age

Table 10

Proportion of Subjects Giving the Specified Number of "Yes" Responses on the CMI, for Four Samples of Women Compared to Female Hotel Residents

No. of "Yes" Responses	307 NY Hosp. Employee "Normals"	328 NY City Ostensibly Healthy	3,014 NY Hospital Patients	343 NY Hosp. Neurotic Patients	8 San Diego Hotel Residents
10 or more	43%	79%	84%	99%	100 %
20 " "	13	51	62	83	75
30°" "	05	30	44	65	67.5
40 " "	02	16	30	49	37.5
50°" "	01	09	18	34	25
60 " "	00	05	10	21	12.5
70 " "	00	02	05	12	12.5

The table reads, for example, at the scoring level of 50: 1% of the New York Hospital "normals," 9% of the New York City ostensibly healthy population, 18% of the New York Hospital patients, and 34% of the New York Hospital neurotic patients gave 50 or more "Yes" answers.

°Suggested critical scoring levels.

cohort tended to mention sensory loss (hearing and eyesight) and trouble with walking as problems. About two-fifths (22 percent) stated that they had no major problems. There was a tendency for persons over sixty-five to report that things were going pretty well. As one older man reported: "I don't know that I really have any [problems]. I'm grateful to be as well as I am."

Approximately three-fourths (N=30) of the respondents had been to the doctor within the past year. In most cases (70 percent) respondents used a general practitioner or "regular doctor." Three went to an eye and ear doctor and three used foot specialists. Other types of health professionals seen included psychiatrist/psychologist (2); orthopedic doctor (1); surgeon (2). Approximately one-fourth (N=11) had been patients in a hospital within the past year. The Veterans Hospital was used most frequently.

Within the past year, two-fifths (N=16) had to stay in their rooms because of illness. Half of those responding stayed in their rooms for over one month. Three persons were essentially bedridden. For half of those who were unable to leave their rooms, friends and hotel managers brought food and supplied other services. Friends were most often mentioned as being helpful and bringing food. In three cases, persons mentioned the hotel manager. A few others mentioned that restaurant waitresses delivered their food—two restaurants in the area provided delivery services. In seven of the cases, persons reported that "nobody" helped them. "I had to go out and get it myself. I think having to go out to get my food kept me sick a lot longer."

Not having enough money was a priority item for 12 percent of the respondents. They tended to be under sixty-five and living in the worst SRO hotels. Two individuals mentioned alcoholism as a major problem in their life. Interpersonal problems were a concern for four of the respondents. One person responded, "I'd like to go back to my second wife, but stepkids are a problem." The manner in which some persons stated that they had no problems emphasized their general level of detachment from others. One man stated, "There are none. I don't give a damn about anything, so nothing is a problem."

We asked persons if there were things about themselves or their living conditions which made life difficult or unpleasant. Over half (N=23) reported that there were things making life difficult. Again, personal health (N=12) was most often mentioned as making life unpleasant. Four persons reported that the hotels and persons living in them made things difficult or unpleasant. One person said, "Living here is depressing because of the low class of people, but it is the cheapest place and it's close to meals." Another man living in a small SRO hotel at the periphery of the study area said, "I have to go three blocks to eat, my legs hurt and going up and down stairs is hard. I could live at the Wells Fargo but the room is so small."

Deteriorating health was the major cause for limiting or curtailing activities. Almost one-half (N=19) had limited their activities within the past year. One person replied, "I can't do anything now that I could do a year ago. All I can do is lay here in bed and wait for the Grim Reaper." Another individual lamented, "I can't pull the knobs on the candy machine. I am too weak." A limitation in walking ability was the most missed activity. "I don't have confidence in walking. I love to walk. The wind hurts my eyes and gives me headaches." Several persons reported that they had given up working within the past year. One member of the fifty to fifty-five year age cohort was in considerable distress over his inability to find a job. "I've given up on myself over a job. It's all mental. I've developed a drinking habit." An eighty-two-year-old man reported a similar distress over inability to work. "I repaired jewelry. I can't do it now. I'm just living from one day to the next now."

Few persons (17 percent) mentioned having problems with living alone. Of the seven people who had difficulty living alone, all had negative self-perceptions of their health and all were men. One sixty-one-year-old man felt that living alone was

> the worst sickness in the world. Have someone around. That's why I have a parakeet. These are the five main things: (1) women, (2) children, (3) animals, (4) good food, (5) music.

While not feeling that living alone created difficulties for them, about one-third (*N*=15) did have spells of loneliness. One person summed up the typical response: "I feel lonely once in awhile. Just like everybody does who lives alone." Some persons had experienced feeling lonely for an extended period of time. One person felt lonely since, "My wife dying in 1964." Another said, "I've felt lonely my entire life."

When asked what kinds of things would help alleviate their loneliness, most respondents wished they could regain something lost, such as, their health, a job, or a relationship. One person stated, "There's no solution for that [loneliness], I'm elderly and it can't be changed." One person had an innovative idea: "I would like to open up a soup kitchen for all us drunks and only charge half price." Loneliness was not related to any of the variables tested (age, education, hotel). However, there was a tendency for more men than women to complain about loneliness and for their self-perception of their health to be negative.

Functional Health Capacity

Downtown hotel residents scored higher on the Index of Incapacity (a measure of functional ability) than the national sample.[28] On the basis of the index score, the national sample group appears healthier and less incapacitated. On the other hand, the San Diego hotel residents showed less functional incapacity than persons living in Chicago residential hotels.[29] (See Table 11 for comparisons.)

Over half (*N*=30; 56 percent) of the San Diego hotel sample were able to function without limitation as measured on the scale. An additional quarter (27 percent) of the sample had scores of one or two—that is, they may have some difficulty with one or two items on the index or may be completely unable to do one item. Thus, four-fifths of the respondents had only minimal functional impairment as measured by the index. However, a considerable portion reported a high level of incapacity on the index; 10 percent of the San Diego sample reported severe limitations as compared to only 1 percent in the national sample. This finding supports field work observations that the SRO hotels in the downtown have an overrepresentation of disabled and physically impaired persons.

Scores on the CMI were compared to scores on the Index of Incapacity (Table 12). Scoring one or more on the Index of Incapacity was significantly related to scoring above the critical level of thirty on the CMI (x^2 = 4.6 p < .05). This relationship held despite the six month time span between the administration of the CMI and the Index of Incapacity. Scores on the Index of Incapacity were not related to age, sex, or education.

Component Parts of the Index of Incapacity

As expected, the ability of old people to function in the six areas covered by the index varied considerably. Some persons had to curtail their outdoor activities and mobility but were able to take care of their own personal needs. Others could do all the tasks except climb up and down stairs. Table 13 gives the percentage of the hotel sample reporting difficulty with common physical tasks and compares them with national averages.

One-fifth (N=8) of the SRO hotel residents had difficulty in going out-of-doors. Chicago hotel residents studied by Bild and Havighurst showed a similar level of difficulty.[30] For some SRO residents, not being able to enjoy the California climate was distressing. In Shanas and Associates' national survey, walking up and down stairs was the most difficult task reported.[31] Walking up and down stairs and cutting toenails were the two most difficult tasks for downtown hotel residents. An equal percentage (29 percent) had difficulty with these two tasks. Two persons reported that they were unable to climb steps at all—one lived in a hotel without an elevator. These persons were shut in and, on this basis alone, ill-housed. The reason why people were not able to use steps varied; some were physically disabled, others had heart trouble or problems with breathing. Cutting their own toenails created problems for

Table 11

Comparison of Index of Incapacity Scores Among Different Groups of Elderly (Percent)

Scores	San Diego Hotels°	U.S. Sample	Persons Living in Resident Hotels in Chicago	
			Uptown	Hyde Park
0	56	68	41	35
1-2	27	21	29	28
3-4	2	6	11	12
5-6	5	4	11	12
7	10	1	9	12

° The San Diego sample included persons aged 50 years and over; however, age was not related to scores on the Index of Incapacity.

Table 12

Comparison of Scores on the CMI with Functional Health Score Downtown San Diego Hotel Residents
($N=75$)

Functional Score	CMI Scores	
	Average	Median
0	27	26
1-6	39	34
7+	43	34

Table 13

**Percentage of Hotel Sample
Reporting Difficulty with
Common Physical Tasks**

Tasks	San Diego Sample $N=41$	National Sample° $N=2,432$
Walking up and down stairs	29	30
Getting about hotel/house	19	6
Washing and bathing	15	10
Dressing and putting on shoes	21	8
Cutting toenails	29	19

Source: E. Shanas, *Old People in Three Industrial Societies.* New York: Atherton, 1968, p. 28.

many residents. Five persons were unable to cut their own toenails. Some had friends or relatives to assist them, a few went to the foot specialist, some did nothing. The reasons for having difficulty in cutting toenails included rheumatism (pain and stiffness), poor eyesight, lack of strength. In comparison to the national sample, San Diego hotel residents had more difficulty in getting around the hotel/house as well as dressing and putting on shoes. Two persons stated that they could only get around inside the hotel with some assistance. Nine persons had difficulty with dressing and putting on shoes; however, none were completely limited in this task. Washing and bathing was the least difficult task for hotel residents to perform. Two persons reported that they could only do this task with the help of others. One person could not get in and out of the bath tub, so took a sponge bath using the sink in her room.

Discussion

As mentioned in Chapter 1, findings on the health of downtown hotel residents are contradictory and paradoxical. Some researchers maintain that older residents in urban hotels and rooming houses are in exceedingly poor physical and emotional health.[32] Others assert that this is a population with low perceived health difficulties.[33] As in many issues of this sort, both sides are in part correct, but overlook aspects of the total picture.

More than anything else, the downtown population is characterized by heterogeneity. This heterogeneity is especially evident when age cohorts are compared. The most consistent finding regarding health status among San Diego hotel residents was the more negative perception of health within the preretirement age cohort (fifty to sixty-four). On the basis of cross-sectional data, it was impossible to determine whether the older cohort's lower CMI scores resulted from adjustment to chronic problems more alarming when they were younger. The data is supportive of one study[34] showing that people who had been afflicted with chronic health problems rated their health better than did individuals who were just beginning to confront such difficulties. Thus, poor perceived health among the younger cohort could result from the emergent awareness of illness and inability to find work. Whatever the case, overall ratings of poor health (both physical and psychiatric) suggested emotional difficulties and problems with adjustment. This finding supported the earlier work of Matarazzo and his associates in 1961 and Lawton, 1959.[35] The older cohort emerge as the survivors—they are the persons who successfully adjusted and resolved mid-life crises.

Overall, it would be incorrect to characterize downtown hotel residents as "exceedingly healthy." Many persons perceive themselves to be getting along quite well, but for the older cohort, this perspective is essential for continued independent living. For this group, denial of bodily and emotional symptoms is a positive adjustment in maintaining self-reliance and an independent lifestyle. In particular, the older cohort has a larger percentage of persons who have led mobile, single lives in the past. They appear to have deliberately chosen (within limits) the central city hotels. They fit the aforementioned life trajectory of lifelong loner.

Most older SRO residents are marginal in terms of their economic resources and social support systems when in crisis. Their lack of connection with kinsmen and friends, plus their avoidance of community agencies and services, contributes to their vulnerability in times of crisis. Short of severe crises, the hotels and their environs provide vital supports and services. As representatives of a distinctive lifestyle, their needs are best met in the hotel's urban context. More in the younger cohort appear to have been forced into the cheap hotels through lack of choice. Their life trajectories frequently demonstrate that of the marginally social adjusted.

Notes

1   R. Dubos, *Man Adapting* (New Haven: Yale University Press, 1965): 346.

2   B. Hoke, "Promotive Medicine and the Phenomenon of Health," *Archives of Environmental Health* 16 (1968): 271.

3   Dubos, *Man Adapting,* 351.

4   This follows the definition by D. Mechanic in *Medical Sociology* (New York: The Free Press, 1968).

5   K. Brodman, A.J. Erdmann, Jr., C.P. Gershenson and H.G. Wolff, "The Cornell Medical Index-Health Questionnaire. III. The Evaluation of Emotional Disturbances," *Journal of Clinical Psychology* (1952): 119-24.

6   A.J.K. Erdmann, I. Brodman, I. Lorge and H.G. Wolff, "The Cornell Medical Index-Health Questionnaire. V. The Outpatient Admitting Department of a General Hospital," *Journal of the American Medical Association* 149 (June 7, 1952):550-51; H. Herbolsheimer and B.L. Ballard, "Multiple Screening in Evaluation of Entering College and University Students," *Journal of the American Medical Association* 166 (February 1, 1958):444-53; M.P. Lawton, "The Screening Value of the Cornell Medical Index," *Journal of Consulting Psychology* 23 (1959):352-56.

7   J.H. Abramson, "The Cornell Medical Index as an Epidemiological Tool," *American Journal of Public Health* 56 (Feb., 1966):287-98.

8   R.T. Monroe, F.E. Whiskin, P. Bonacich and W.O. Jewell, III, "The Cornell Medical Index Questionnaire as a Measure of Health in Older People," *Journal of Gerontology* 20 (January, 1965):18-22; R.W. Steinhardt, F.D. Zeman, J. Tuchman and I. Lorge, "Appraisal of Physical and Mental Health of the Elderly; Use of Cornell Medical Index and Supplementary Health Questionnaire," *Journal of the American Medical Association* 151 (January, 1953):378-82.

9   Abramson, "Epidemiological Tool"; Monroe, et. al., "Measure of Health in Older People."

10   Abramson, "Epidemiological Tool," 29.

11   Ibid., 292.

12   E.A. Kark, A. Zaslany and B. Ward, "The Health of the Undergraduate Student on Entry to the Hebrew University in Jerusalem," *Israel Medical Journal* 22 (1963): 147-155; N.A. Scotch and H.J. Geiger, "An Index of Symptoms and Disease in Zulu Culture," *Human Organization* 22 (1963-64):304-11; L.G. Laufer, "Cultural Problems Encountered in Use of the Cornell Index Among Okinawan Natives," *American Journal of Psychiatry* 109 (1953):861-864; N.A. Chance, "Conceptual and Methodological Problems in Cross-Cultural Health Research," *American Journal of Public Health* 52 (1962):410-17.

13   S.H. Croog, "Educational Level and Responses to a Health Questionnaire," *Human Organization* 20 (1961):65-69.

14   Kark et al., "Health of Undergraduate Students"; Scotch and Geiger, "Disease in Zulu Culture"; K. Brodman, A.J. Erdmann, Jr., I. Lorge and H.W. Wolff, "The Cornell Medical Index-Health Questionnaire. VI. The Relation of Patients' Complaints to Age, Sex, Race, and Education," *Journal of Gerontology* 8 (1953):339-42.

15   Croog, "Educational Level."

16   J. Cassel and H.A. Tyroler, "Epidemiological Studies of Culture
          Change: I. Health Status and Recency of Industrialization," *Archives
          of Environmental Health* 3 (1961):25-33.

17   P. Townsend, "Measuring Incapacity for Self-Care," in *Processes of
          Aging,* II, ed. R.H. Williams, C. Tibbitts and W. Donahue (New York:
          Atherton Press, 1963), p. 272.

18   Ibid.

19   E. Shanas, P. Townsend, D. Wedderburn, H. Friis, P. Milhoj and J.
          Stehouwer (eds.), *Old People in Three Industrial Societies* (New York:
          Atherton, 1968).

20   Ibid., 27.

21   P. Haberman, "The Reliability and Validity of the Data," in *Poverty
          and Health,* ed. J. Kosa, et. al. (Cambridge: Harvard University Press,
          1969).

22   Most notably, G.L. Maddox, "Self Assessment of Health Status: A
          Longitudinal Study of Elderly Subjects," *Journal of Chronic Diseases*
          17 (1964):449-460; G.L. Maddox and E.B. Douglas, "Self Assessment
          of Health: A Longitudinal Study of Elderly Subjects, *Journal of Health
          and Social Behavior* 14(1973):18-93.

23   Ibid., 88.

24   Ibid., 92.

25   P. Ehrlich, *St. Louis' "Invisible" Elderly: Needs and Characteristics of
          Aged "Single Room Occupancy" Downtown Hotel Residents* (St.
          Louis: Institute of Applied Gerontology, St. Louis University, 1976);
          B.J. Stephens, *Loners, Losers, and Lovers: Elderly Tenants in a Slum
          Hotel* (Seattle: University of Washington Press, 1976).

26   In another study of the SRO population conducted by WBSI, 82 hotel
          residents were asked to whom they would turn in eleven different
          situations. The most frequent response was that they could turn "to no
          one." After turning "to no one," hotel residents relied on friends inside
          the hotel or to hotel employees for assistance. In response to the

question, "Do you get any kind of help from your family?" 72 percent of the residents said they got no kind of help from family. When asked, "Would you like help?" 75 percent said "No" (R.J. Erickson and J.K. Eckert, "The Elderly Poor in Downtown San Diego Hotels," *Gerontologist* 17, no. 5 (1977): 440-446.

27   J. Martin and A. Doran, "Perception of Retirement: Time and Season," Pilkington Research Project on Retirement, Liverpool, England; J.M. Mulanaphy, "1972-73 Survey of Retired TIAA-CREF Annuitants," Statistical Report, Teachers Insurance and Annuity Association, College Retirement Equities Fund (New York, 1974); C. Ryser and A. Shelton, "Retirement and Health," *Journal of American Geriatric Society* 17 (1969):180-190; W.E. Thompson and G.F. Streib, "Situational Determinants: Health and Economic Deprivation in Retirement," *Journal of Social Issues* 14, no. 2 (1958):18-34.

28   Shanas et al. *Old People.*

29   B. Bild and R. Havighurst, "Senior Citizens in Great Cities: The Case of Chicago," *The Gerontologist* 16, no. 1, Part II (1976) 56.

30   Ibid.

31   Shanas et al. *Old People.*

32   J.H. Shapiro, *Communities of the Alone* (New York: Association Press, 1971); H. Siegal, *Outposts of the Forgotten: Lifeways of Socially Terminal People in Slum Hotels and Single Room Occupancy Tenements* (New Jersey: Transaction Books, 1978); Stephens, *Loners, Losers, and Lovers.*

33   Ehrlich, *St. Louis' "Invisible" Elderly;* T. Tissue, "Old Age, Poverty and the Central City," *Aging and Human Development* 2 (1971):235-48.

34   E. Shanas, *The Health of Older People: A Social Survey* (Cambridge: Harvard University Press, 1962).

35   R.G. Matarazzo, J.D. Matarazzo and G. Saslow, "The Relationships Between Medical and Psychiatric Systems," *Journal of Abnormal and Social Psychology* 62 (1961):55-61; M.P. Lawton, "The Screening Value of the Cornell Medical Index," *Journal of Consulting Psychology* 23 (1959):352-56.

11

Summary and Conclusions

This study explores one living alternative available to older persons in urban areas: single room occupancy hotels. In San Diego, these hotels are located in the deteriorated urban core of San Diego, an area which is described as the "skid row" or "tenderloin." Both symbolically and physically, the area is similar to deteriorated zones in other American cities. With this symbolic identity, south of Broadway becomes a geographic locale and human condition characterized by people living on minimal incomes, outside "typical" family relationships, in low-cost single room arrangements.

While this study focuses on an ethnographic description of the SRO hotel setting, it has also considered in some depth the mental and physical health status of the older residents. Health status as a substantive issue for older residents grows out of the ethnographic description of the hotels. From this perspective health is viewed in the context of the individual's interdependencies with his environment. The older hotel residents are not viewed apart from their surroundings, but instead in the context of a physical and social environment—a milieu which is capable of hindering or facilitating their ability to adjust and adapt.

The goals of the study have been: to conduct a naturalistic field study of older persons living in center city hotels; to explore the primary social divisions and groups within the hotel setting; to gain an understanding of the values, problems, and needs of the older residents themselves; to determine the self-perceived health status and functional ability of these tough urban dwellers.

A multimethodological approach incorporating participant observation with structured and unstructured interviewing was employed to discover interactional patterns and their maintenance, dominant values, empirical data on general health status of the population, and the patterning of life of the older residents.

In San Diego's downtown there are several types of living arrangements available to older persons. They range from senior citizen high-rises to rooming houses and hotels. Within the category of hotels there are several variations. There are large commercial hotels, specialty retirement hotels and single room occupancy hotels which offer furnished rooms at relatively inexpensive rates. Single room occupancy hotels vary along the dimensions of size, enforcement of rules and regulations, and preferred clientele.

The hotels selected for this study vary in size from 12 to 325 rooms and in degree of behavioral permissiveness. They are similar in that their dominant clientele are older persons, mostly male, living on fixed incomes near the poverty line. This particular group is frequently lumped together with "undersirable" categories of people in the urban core. Middle class planners and developers do not like the areas in which such people live — there is a tendency to view everyone in the same negative way and want to "clean it up." This position fails to recognize the critical differences and needs of diverse populations. Many elderly hotel dwellers have found a lifestyle that suits them. They might like a more pleasant room and perhaps better food, but not at the cost of their capacity to make choices and remain independent.

The SRO hotel dweller represents an unseen population about which little is known, for research on their lifestyle has only begun to emerge. These elderly residents are unseen and ignored by the masses who enter the city for work or play and return to their suburban communities. Yet these older residents represent the true urban dweller. On the whole, they prefer the urban environment and rely on it to meet their daily needs.

Meeting the Basic Physical and Social Needs of Residents

Urban Hotels. The urban commercial zone and hotels supply the older residents with important services to meet their daily needs. The most important feature of the environment is the hotel itself. Within the hotel one is able to rent a furnished room with linens, heat, housekeeping services, and a modicum of security. In the Ballentine hotel, the primary hotel for ethnographic consideration, a full range of staff and housekeeping services were offered. The hotel had a lobby, T.V. room, and elevator — all of which were important to the older residents.

The Ballentine represents the norm in the continuum of SRO hotels in the downtown San Diego area. It is average in the number of rooms, rates, permissiveness, ratio of young to old, and transients to permanents. The percentage of female residents is slightly higher than is typical for other SRO hotels in the area. Like many other hotels in downtown San Diego, the Ballentine has a heterogeneous population, but is dominated by the presence of older retirees. Interspersed with the older permanent residents are transients of all ages. The transients include Navy men on shore leave, pimps and prostitutes, the unemployed, alcoholics and drug addicts. The social boundaries between the older permanents and these subgroups are distinct with little social interaction taking place.

Hotels vary in the level of permissive behavior they allow. Those that are very permissive are not attractive to the majority of older retirees. Some level of disruptive behavior is tolerable, but older tenants value managers and staff that are "hard nosed" and look out for them. At the Ballentine policies change in response to economics, new staff, and the mood of the management. There are certain periods where tenants are scrutinized and potential trouble makers are turned away or evicted. At other times policies regarding tenants loosen up and rooms are rented to almost anyone.

Hotels also vary in the percentage of residents with serious mental and physical health problems. For example, some hotels are consistently permissive and rent to known alcoholics and drug users. At the Ballentine, some effort was made not to rent to persons with potentially disruptive problems. Although some older residents in the Ballentine suffered from alcoholism, the majority had difficulties with chronic conditions including hearing and vision loss, heart trouble, emphysema, and stroke. Even though the older hotel residents have numerous health problems, they still manage to care for themselves. The high value placed on independence makes functional health a prerequisite for successful hotel living.

Infrastructure of Services. Enhancing the attractiveness of the downtown area to the older retiree is the large number of cheap restaurants in which it is possible to get a balanced diet. It is typical for the older resident to eat twice a day; breakfast sometime in the morning and a mid-afternoon dinner. The procurement of food is a dominant rhythm in everyday life. Some persons choose to cook one of their daily meals on hot plates in their rooms. However, the preparation of meals is complicated by the paucity of reasonably priced grocery stores in the downtown.

Older residents in the hotels buy secondhand clothing at the Sally (Salvation Army) or Volunteers (of America). Such clothes are necessary in order to dress one's identity.[1] When one is "properly" dressed, one is identifiable as a resident, and hence is not hassled as a visitor may be.

A number of other services are readily available in the downtown which help meet the physical needs of the elderly residents. There are discount drug stores in which to buy medicine, sundries, shaving needs and the like. Laundromats are available in the area and some hotels have their own laundry machines. Police and other safety provisions are close at hand.

The urban zone further provides transportation that is both accessible and affordable. An interesting service and one which was important to many of the older men was an inexpensive barber college in the area. Since the students needed subjects on which to practice, haircuts and shaves were given at minimal cost; some at no cost. As a result, some men would go two or three times a week for their shaves.

Underlying all these requirements is the need for an income. The income of older residents is derived largely from Social Security. A few of the residents have military or work pensions. Some get SSI (supplementary security income) from the state and in a few cases men below the age of sixty-two receive welfare payments. Some older hotel residents are able to supplement their incomes through other means. Informally arranged part-time jobs in local shops provide a small portion of the residents with extra money. Some others obtain supplementary money and goods through a variety of unconventional means including (1) "go-fors"; (2) "conning"; (3) "scavenging"; and (4) "borrowing." Taken together, unconventional strategies for making money are less elaborate among San Diego SRO hotel residents than similar persons in larger and more hostile environments.

Social Structure and Social Support. The hotels provide the basic social structure and means of support for the older residents. It is itself a social group, with statuses and roles. Given the services of the hotel and a steady, though minimal income, the residents can lead the rest of their social lives with any person or group they choose to find. What is important, is the belief among residents that they do have some choice. The hotel environment provides the setting for as much or as little social interaction as one desires. If one chooses to keep to oneself, there is little or no social pressure or censure for that behavior. In like fashion, if one chooses to interact with others the opportunities are ever present. Most residents choose a set of dyadic relationships[2] that are for the most part superficial and utilitarian. The relationships frequently revolve around discussing sports, politics, and gambling.

A few of the residents are able to establish cross-sex dyadic relationships. Quite frequently these relationships do not involve sex; more typically, the woman will be in a position of providing helping services to a less dependent male. Unlike most other settings with large concentrations of older persons, women are few in SRO hotels, yet they are visible for the social glue they provide. Women, more than men, are engaged in social networks and supportive arrangements. They frequently supply a caretaking function to each other and to some male hotel residents. They are no less self-reliant and independent than are the men. In general, social interactions among women are similar to those found among men. They are characterized by a lack of trust and a superficiality in content. Both men and women value their privacy and freedom. The most important dimension of friendship involves utilitarian helping relationships. Furthermore, while older hotel residents have numerous acquaintances, those considered intimate friends are very few in number. Primary and supportive relationships with kinsmen are underdeveloped. Contacts with kinsmen are infrequent and few older residents say they rely on them in crisis situations.

A series of dyadic relationships forms the social network of each resident. The simplicity of the social structure is evident not only in the shallow content of the dyadic relationships, but in the small number of them.[3] The duration of each social interaction tends to be brief, and the frequency is not very great. The links in the network contain few people, and most of them are single-stranded. Few networks include kinsmen. The number of people in one's network who know one another (density) is not very high, and the degree of connection is small.

Some social groups do form among hotel residents. In the Ballentine, small groups or cliques formed around activities such as watching the television or discussing sports and politics. Some residents who did not participate in such cliques viewed them with disdain. One nonparticipating older resident told me, "I like to stay clear of those lobby lizards." Where social groups do evolve, they are based on common interests and especially long-term residence. Again, it is interesting to note that most of the social groups that do form have at least one woman in them who acts as a kind of social cement. On the whole, these groups are ephemeral and of limited function.

Most older retirees choose to handle their own problems, yet hotel staff are important. The hotel staff, which includes managers, desk clerks, and maids, frequently take a benevolent attitude toward the older residents and provide services of a nonpersonal and pragmatic nature. Managers and desk clerks help residents by extending credit, making loans, taking messages, giving advice, screening visitors, etc. In general, maids "keep an eye" on the older residents. They are on the separate floors of the hotel each day and have the opportunity to check on residents and note changes in their personal habits (e.g., becoming ill or bedridden, drinking excessively). Since the hotels serve as an important source of formal and informal secondary support, the residents are not required to create a further social network in order to get many of their needs fulfilled. Living in the hotels provides older residents with a ready and available helping network and contributes to a psychological sense of wellbeing. Services such as these are available at a monthly cost that the older residents can afford. If similar caretaking was formally supplied through social service programs the cost no doubt would be much higher.

Other caretakers are external to the hotels. A portion can be referred to as the "anonymous service fringe." For some hotel residents, service personnel (shopkeepers, bank tellers, waitresses, postal clerks) offer a structure for social relationships. They personalize the relationships with them to meet their own needs. Not all relationships with the anonymous service fringe are positive. Many of the bureaucratized social/ health agencies are viewed negatively and avoided whenever possible. In particular, the state and federal "welfare" systems are stigmatized and avoided. Older hotel residents frequently view health-oriented caretakers, including hospitals and doctors, as being primarily interested in the "medicine buck" and not in their wellbeing.

Many residents are forced to rely on what they say is "depersonalized and third rate" health care offered by the county and local V.A. hospitals. Because of the strong negative feelings associated with these and other health services, older retirees tend to deny medical problems until they become incapacitating. What results is a further reliance on the depersonalized crisis care offered by local hospital emergency rooms and outpatient clinics.

The Life Patterns and Dominant Values of Older Residents

The life histories and adjustments of SRO hotel residents follow several identifiable trajectories or patterns. Three broad patterns of life adjustment are discernible: (1) the lifelong loner; (2) the retreatist or marginally socially adjusted; (3) the late isolate. In the case of the lifelong loner and retreatist, there is a pattern of rejecting intimacy and conventional roles of husband or wife, mother or father, and community member. Late isolates are quite different from either the lifelong loner or retreatist, yet the resulting anonymity is the same. These persons are alone because they have outlived their friends and significant relatives. They tend to be the old, old (seventy-five plus). For them, living in cheap hotels on a minimal income is a negative result of the aging process. However, even in the cases where children would take them in, they choose to preserve their autonomy and independence by continuing to live in the hotels. Regardless of their past histories, older residents view the hotels as superior to more structured institutions.

For most older SRO residents there is a long ingrained impulse toward autonomy and self-reliance. Among the present older generation of men and women in our culture, and especially the predominantly male culture of the SRO, the ability to keep on managing for oneself, to make it alone, to reaffirm that one is still self-governing is of the utmost importance. The need to uphold the principle of self-reliance demands that older residents do not appear as the "weak" member of a dyad. Thus some do not take the help that they can get because to do so is to admit weakness. What the older residents avoid are situations in which they are involved in nonreciprocal roles. In nonreciprocal situations they consider themselves dependent, since they have nothing they consider of value to give in return for whatever help they get. In Clark's terms, they fear that other people will see their dependency as neurotic dependency.[4] Under such a condition their self-image suffers.

Older individuals are variably successful in their ability to "fit" into the SRO setting. To a large degree, success is dependent upon how closely one's lifelong trajectory pattern approximates that of a lifelong loner. The best suited are those who accept and value privacy, freedom, minimal authority with few social demands and responsibilities, and an all male setting. The less well adapted are those persons who have tried a conventional life and failed. For them living in the hotel environment is vivid proof of their failure to achieve a middle class life-style.

The Major Threat to Autonomy: Deteriorating Health and Functional Ability

On the whole, older hotel dwellers are in worse health than age peers in other settings. As described in the previous chapter, there is a high level of perceived physical and emotional complaints. Health findings show that the older post-retirement cohort had near normal self-perceptions of health while the younger preretirement group perceived themselves to be in poorer health. While many in the older cohort were realistic and even optimistic about their health, persons in the younger cohort were often pessimistic not only about their health, but their life situation in general. However, even the older groups (sixty-five plus), when compared to a national sample of age peers, showed a higher level of functional impairment than expected. Thus, findings did not support the belief of some researchers that downtown men were exceptionally healthy.[5]

While the overall level of disability among older SRO residents is high, those in the older cohort (sixty-five plus) deny many of their problems and minimize their needs. They avoid potential "helpers" from outside the hotel environment. They fear that the outside helpers (including social/health professionals and relatives) in their efforts to provide assistance, will fail to honor or somehow undermine their needs for independence, self-reliance, and a modicum of control over their own lives.

Older hotel residents are adjusted as long as they are capable of acting in accordance with the norms of their milieu. Since a wide spectrum of behavior and eccentricities is allowable in many SRO hotels, only in the most extreme cases of acting out, alcholism, and disability are sanctions brought down on residents.

In terms of adaptation (the ability to get along well enough with society and oneself to preserve intact the personal functions) some hotel residents are not doing very well. While they remain adjusted in the sense that they can continue to live in the hotels, they are maladapted in the sense that they are depressed, have negative views of themselves, and are in a fragile balance with their social world. For example, some persons avoid conflict with society by an escape into anonymity and isolation. Others who are in poor functional health remain isolated and anonymous so as not to be "discovered" by social service professionals or relatives who, in the process of helping, might rob them of their autonomy.

In particular, functional health emerges as the critical variable for the older SRO residents' continued successful adjustment to the hotels. Declining functional health (i.e., the ability to cope with getting one's own food and do the other things necessary to keep going) is the most critical and threatening factor affecting the life of the SRO resident.

Adaptations to marginal economic resources, loss of work, and loss of social ties (if they ever existed) are all possible if functional health is maintained. When asked, many older respondents report a high level of medical complaints and symptoms, but as long as the symptoms do not result in severe functional incapacity, they can continue to perceive themselves as getting along quite well.

When functional difficulties become too severe and can no longer be denied or hidden from the view of hotel staff and neighbors, institutionalization is the only remaining option. At this stage "help" frequently becomes a serious threat. To avoid the inevitable, some refuse to be admitted for hospital care or any kind of formal help for as long as possible. What results is a sort of voluntary suicide. Some older residents would rather die alone in their rooms than admit the loss of independence by accepting hospitalization or institutionalization.

The resemblance of complete self-reliance is exceedingly important for the older SRO resident. Residents who can sustain the image of complete self-reliance and independence seem to have higher morale and self-esteem than those who cannot. Even though some may be lonely and in need, they are at least remaining true to their ideals and values.

On the basis of the total protocol it appears that the younger cohort (aged fifty to sixty-five) lives in the hotels for reasons of unemployment, alcoholism, marital discord, injuries, accidents, and other disabilities. The younger cohort seems more receptive to outside help and whatever benefits are obtainable. The older group attaches more stigma to any help or benefit that connotes "welfare." They rely more heavily on the informal supports offered by hotel staff and community services, including transportation and convenience to shops and restaurants. These supports are viewed as nonthreatening to their autonomy. Within the hotel setting the older SRO resident can find persons with whom to negotiate informal social exchanges for help and services.

A Need for Understanding and Action

Many of the numerous living environments in which people live are either not understood or misunderstood by people from other niches of society. Those persons with minimal economic resources, who are old, and who live in our center cities are among the most misunderstood. The tendency to concentrate on social disorganization and deviant behavior in urban settings has helped to stigmatize its residents. The end result is that areas are targeted for destruction, some for renewal and redevelopment, others for parking lots and highways. More often than not, such decisions are made with little or no consideration for the people who might be directly affected.

For the older hotel resident, the decision to live in the downtown area is one of choice. Inexpensive hotel rooms and the provision of housekeeping services, coupled with the availability of needed goods and services, make the downtown hotels a practical alternative. Additionally, hotels are semi-institutional in character and offer numerous supportive services for residents at a price, and in some cases, with a finesse that is not available in many formal "extended" care facilities. Unlike extended care facilities, hotels supply continual supervision in the forms of clerks, maids, and other residents while allowing for freedom of choice in the activities of daily living.

The data support the notion of a distinctive lifestyle based on an "alone" pattern of living in rented rooms. Within the hotels is a large percentage of persons who have led mobile, single lives in the past and seem to prefer living alone in the present. While they do not romanticize hotel life, they overwhelmingly prefer it to any form of "institutional" living for older adults. Planners and professionals, in their efforts to support and improve the quality of life, must honor the rights of hotel dwellers to choose their own style of life.

An important message and perhaps the central message of this book is that we seek to understand and support the cultural diversity in this country. This understanding is absolutely vital if we are to maintain the rich variety of lifestyles we find around us. We cannot make plans to redevelop or change living environments until we have some understanding of their complexity, function, and cost to life.

Notes

1   L.H. Lofland, *A World of Strangers* (New York: Basic Books, 1973).

2   The dyad is the simplest social "group" because only two people are involved: It can be kept to a single set of roles in a single social context. Such dyadic relationships need not be multiplex; they need make no enduring social demands. The content of these relationships is usually limited to the exchange of brief conversations and occasional jokes. They may exchange small money loans, nods, or helping services in times of illness or bad luck. See P.J. Bohannan, "A Room of My Own," unpublished manuscript, 1977.

3   Ibid.

4   M. Clark, "Cultural Values and Dependency in Later Life," in *Aging and Modernization*, ed. D.O. Cowgill and L.D. Holmes (New York: Appleton-Century Crofts, 1972), p. 273.

5   P. Ehrlich, *St. Louis "Invisible" Elderly: Needs and Characteristics of Aged "Single Room Occupancy" Downtown Hotel Residents* (St. Louis: Institute of Applied Gerontology, St. Louis University, 1976); T. Tissue, "Old Age, Poverty and the Central City," *Aging and Human Development* 2 (1971):235-48.

Appendix

Western Behavioral Sciences Institute
1150 Silverado Street
La Jolla, CA 92037
(714) 459-3811
1/76

Interviewer _____

Date of Interview _____

Respondent ID No. _____

Hotel ID No. _____

Panel Interview No.   1   2   3   4   5
                          (circle one)

Unseen Community Project: Cornell Medical Index
Downtown Hotel Residence

Office Check—put initials

Completeness _____
Coded _____
Reliability _____

Unseen Panel Interview

1.   How long have you lived in the downtown San Diego area?

            _____ Years
            _____ Months

2.   How long have you lived in this hotel?

            _____ Years
            _____ Months

3.   Why don't you live north of Broadway?

    3A.   Are there any other reasons?

4.   Who would you most likely talk to about an illness you had before seeking professional medical care?

            _____ Relative
            _____ Friend in the hotel
            _____ Friend outside the hotel
            _____ No one
            _____ Stranger
            _____ Other (specify)

5.   Where do you first go when you are sick?

            _____ Private physician
            _____ Senior Citizen clinic/10th and C
            _____ Free Clinic for Senior Citizens/4th Street
            _____ Hospital Outpatient
            _____ Hospital Emergency Room
            _____ Other (specify)

    5A.   What other places have you gone?

6. How do you pay for your hospital care?

    _____ Personal finances
    _____ MediCare
    _____ MediCal
    _____ Other insurances
    _____ Other sources
    _____ Never in hospital

7. How do you pay for your doctor visits?

    _____ Personal finances
    _____ MediCare
    _____ MediCal
    _____ Other insurances
    _____ Other sources
    _____ Never go to the doctor

8. How do you pay for your prescriptions?

    _____ Personal finances
    _____ MediCare
    _____ MediCal
    _____ Other insurances
    _____ Other sources
    _____ Don't have any prescriptions

9. How old are you?

10. How much education do you have? *(Circle highest grade completed.)*

Grades	1	2	3	4	5	6	7	8
High School	1	2	3	4				
College or University	1	2	3	4	+			

11. What is your marital status? *(Just check answer without asking, if you know.)*

        _____ Married
        _____ Single/Never Married
        _____ Divorced
        _____ Separated
        _____ Widowed
        _____ Other (specify)

11A. *If married before, ask:* How many times have you been married previously?

12. Are you employed?

        _____ Yes
        _____ No
     If no, go to Question 13.

12A. *If yes, ask:* What do you do? What are your job duties? *(Get details)*

12B. Is it full-time or part-time?

        _____ Full-time
        _____ Part-time

12C. *If no, ask:* Are you looking for work?

        _____ Yes
        _____ No
        _____ Other (specify)

12D. Can you tell me a little about your employment history? What things have you done? For how long at a time?

        _____ Never worked

13. What is the source of your income?

14. How much total monthly income do you have to live on—whatever the source?

        $ _____

15. What is your nationality?

    (Interviewer): If they say American, write that but then ask: Where were your parents or grandparents from?

16. Now I have a number of questions about health that I would like to ask you.

Interview ID No. _____

Directions: If you can answer YES to the question asked, put a circle around the YES. If you have to answer NO to the question asked, put a circle around the NO. Answer all questions. If you are not sure, guess.

Section A

1.	Do you need glasses to read?	Yes	No
2.	Do you need glasses to see things at a distance?	Yes	No
3.	Has your eyesight often blacked out completely?	Yes	No
4.	Do your eyes continually blink or water?	Yes	No
5.	Do you often have bad pains in your eyes?	Yes	No
6.	Are your eyes often red or inflamed?	Yes	No
7.	Are you hard of hearing?	Yes	No
8.	Have you ever had a bad running ear?	Yes	No
9.	Do you have constant noises in your ears?	Yes	No

Section B

10.	Do you have to clear your throat frequently?	Yes	No
11.	Do you often feel a choking lump in your throat?	Yes	No
12.	Are you often troubled with bad spells of sneezing?	Yes	No
13.	Is your nose continually stuffed up?	Yes	No
14.	Do you suffer from a constantly running nose?	Yes	No
15.	Have you at times had bad nose bleeds?	Yes	No
16.	Do you often catch severe colds?	Yes	No
17.	Do you frequently suffer from heavy chest colds?	Yes	No

18.	When you catch a cold, do you always have to go to bed?	Yes	No
19.	Do frequent colds keep you miserable all winter?	Yes	No
20.	Do you get hay fever?	Yes	No
21.	Do you suffer from asthma?	Yes	No
22.	Are you troubled by constant coughing?	Yes	No
23.	Have you ever coughed up blood?	Yes	No
24.	Do you sometimes have severe soaking sweats at night?	Yes	No
25.	Have you ever had a chronic chest condition?	Yes	No
26.	Have you ever had T.B. (Tuberculosis)?	Yes	No
27.	Did you ever live with anyone who had T.B.?	Yes	No

Section C

28.	Has a doctor ever said your blood pressure was too high?	Yes	No
29.	Has a doctor ever said your blood pressure was too low?	Yes	No
30.	Do you have pains in the heart or chest?	Yes	No
31.	Are you often bothered by thumping of the heart?	Yes	No
32.	Does your heart often race like mad?	Yes	No
33.	Do you often have difficulty in breathing?	Yes	No
34.	Do you get out of breath long before anyone else?	Yes	No
35.	Do you sometimes get out of breath just sitting still?	Yes	No
36.	Are your ankles often badly swollen?	Yes	No
37.	Do cold hands or feet trouble you even in hot weather?	Yes	No
38.	Do you suffer from frequent cramps in your legs?	Yes	No
39.	Has a doctor ever said you had heart trouble?	Yes	No
40.	Does heart trouble run in your family?	Yes	No

Section D

41.	Have you lost more than half your teeth?	Yes	No
42.	Are you troubled by bleeding gums?	Yes	No
43.	Have you often had severe toothaches?	Yes	No
44.	Is your tongue usually badly coated?	Yes	No
45.	Is your appetite always poor?	Yes	No
46.	Do you usually eat sweets or other food between meals?	Yes	No
47.	Do you always gulp your food in a hurry?	Yes	No
48.	Do you often suffer from an upset stomach?	Yes	No
49.	Do you usually feel bloated after eating?	Yes	No
50.	Do you usually belch a lot after eating?	Yes	No
51.	Are you often sick to your stomach?	Yes	No
52.	Do you suffer from indigestion?	Yes	No
53.	Do severe pains in the stomach often double you up?	Yes	No
54.	Do you suffer from constant stomach trouble?	Yes	No

55.	Does stomach trouble run in your family?	Yes	No
56.	Has a doctor ever said you had stomach ulcers?	Yes	No
57.	Do you suffer from frequent loose bowel movements?	Yes	No
58.	Have you ever had severe bloody diarrhea?	Yes	No
59.	Were you ever troubled with intestinal worms?	Yes	No
60.	Do you constantly suffer from bad constipation?	Yes	No
61.	Have you ever had piles (rectal hemorrhoids?)	Yes	No
62.	Have you ever had jaundice (yellow eyes and skin)?	Yes	No
63.	Have you ever had serious liver or gall bladder trouble?	Yes	No

Section E

64.	Are your joints often painfully swollen?	Yes	No
65.	Do your muscles and joints constantly feel stiff?	Yes	No
66.	Do you usually have severe pains in the arms or legs?	Yes	No
67.	Are you crippled with severe rheumatism (arthritis)?	Yes	No
68.	Does rheumatism (arthritis) run in your family?	Yes	No
69.	Do weak or painful feet make your life miserable?	Yes	No
70.	Do pains in the back make it hard for you to keep up with your work?	Yes	No
71.	Are you troubled with serious bodily disability or deformity?	Yes	No

Section F

72.	Is your skin very sensitive or tender?	Yes	No
73.	Do cuts in your skin usually stay open a long time?	Yes	No
74.	Does your face often get badly flushed?	Yes	No
75.	Do you sweat a great deal even in cold weather?	Yes	No
76.	Are you often bothered by severe itching?	Yes	No
77.	Does your skin often break out in a rash?	Yes	No
78.	Are you often troubled with boils?	Yes	No

Section G

79.	Do you suffer badly from frequent severe heacaches?	Yes	No
80.	Does pressure or pain in the head often make life miserable?	Yes	No
81.	Are headaches common in your family?	Yes	No
82.	Do you have hot or cold spells?	Yes	No
83.	Do you often have spells of severe dizziness?	Yes	No
84.	Do you frequently feel faint?	Yes	No
85.	Have you fainted more than twice in your life?	Yes	No
86.	Do you have constant numbness or tingling in any part of your body?	Yes	No

87.	Was any part of your body ever paralyzed?	Yes	No
88.	Were you ever knocked unconscious?	Yes	No
89.	Have you at times had a twitching of the face, head or shoulders?	Yes	No
90.	Did you ever have a fit or convulsion (epilepsy)?	Yes	No
91.	Has anyone in your family ever had fits or convulsions (epilepsy)?	Yes	No
92.	Do you bite your nails badly?	Yes	No
93.	Are you troubled by stuttering or stammering?	Yes	No
94.	Are you a sleep walker?	Yes	No
95.	Are you a bed wetter?	Yes	No
96.	Were you a bed wetter between the ages of 8 and 14?	Yes	No

Section H

For Women Only

97.	Have your menstrual periods usually been painful?	Yes	No
98.	Have you often felt weak or sick with your periods?	Yes	No
99.	Have you often had to lie down when your periods came on?	Yes	No
100.	Have you usually been tense or jumpy with your periods?	Yes	No
101.	Have you ever had constant severe hot flashes and sweats?	Yes	No
102.	Have you often been troubled with a vaginal discharge?	Yes	No

For Men Only

97.	Have you ever had anything seriously wrong with your genitals (privates)?	Yes	No
98.	Are your genitals often painful or sore?	Yes	No
99.	Have you ever had treatment for your genitals?	Yes	No
100.	Has a doctor ever said you had a hernia (rupture)?	Yes	No
101.	Have you ever passed blood while urinating (passing water)?	Yes	No
102.	Do you have trouble starting your stream when urinating?	Yes	No
103.	Do you have to get up every night and urinate?	Yes	No
104.	During the day, do you usually have to urinate frequently?	Yes	No
105.	Do you often have severe burning pain when you urinate?	Yes	No
106.	Do you sometimes lose control of your bladder?	Yes	No
107.	Has a doctor ever said you had kidney or bladder disease?	Yes	No

Section I

108.	Do you often get spells of complete exhaustion or fatigue?	Yes	No
109.	Does working tire you out completely?	Yes	No
110.	Do you usually get up tired and exhausted in the morning?	Yes	No
111.	Does every little effort wear you out?	Yes	No
112.	Are you constantly too tired and exhausted even to eat?	Yes	No
113.	Do you suffer from severe nervous exhaustion?	Yes	No
114.	Does nervous exhaustion run in your family?	Yes	No

Section J

115.	Are you frequently ill?	Yes	No
116.	Are you frequently confined to bed by illness?	Yes	No
117.	Are you always in poor health?	Yes	No
118.	Are you considered a sickly person?	Yes	No
119.	Do you come from a sickly family?	Yes	No
120.	Do severe pains and aches make it impossible for you to do your work?	Yes	No
121.	Do you wear yourself out worrying about your health?	Yes	No
122.	Are you always ill and unhappy?	Yes	No
123.	Are you constantly made miserable by poor health?	Yes	No

Section K

124.	Did you ever have scarlet fever?	Yes	No
125.	As a child, did you have rheumatic fever, growing pains or twitching of the limbs?	Yes	No
126.	Did you ever have malaria?	Yes	No
127.	Were you ever treated for severe anemia (thin blood)?	Yes	No
128.	Were you ever treated for "bad blood" (venereal disease)?	Yes	No
129.	Do you have diabetes (sugar disease)?	Yes	No
130.	Did a doctor ever say you had a goiter (in your neck)	Yes	No
131.	Did a doctor ever treat you for tumor or cancer?	Yes	No
132.	Do you suffer from any chronic disease?	Yes	No
133.	Are you definitely underweight?	Yes	No
134.	Are you definitely overweight?	Yes	No
135.	Did a doctor ever say you had varicose veins (swollen veins) in your legs?	Yes	No
136.	Did you ever have a serious operation?	Yes	No
137.	Did you ever have a serious injury?	Yes	No
138.	Do you often have small accidents or injuries?	Yes	No

Section L

139.	Do you usually have great difficulty in falling asleep or staying asleep?	Yes	No
140.	Do you find it impossible to take a regular rest period each day?	Yes	No
141.	Do you find it impossible to take regular daily exercise?	Yes	No
142.	Do you smoke more than 20 cigarettes a day?	Yes	No
143.	Do you drink more than six cups of coffee or tea a day?	Yes	No
144.	Do you usually take two or more alcoholic drinks a day?	Yes	No

Section M

145.	Do you sweat or tremble a lot during examinations or questioning?	Yes	No
146.	Do you get nervous and shaky when approached by a superior?	Yes	No
147.	Does your work fall to pieces when the boss or a superior is watching you?	Yes	No
148.	Does your thinking get completely mixed up when you have to do things quickly?	Yes	No
149.	Must you do things very slowly in order to do them without mistakes?	Yes	No
150.	Do you always get directions and orders wrong?	Yes	No
151.	Do strange people or places make you afraid?	Yes	No
152.	Are you scared to be alone when there are no friends near you?	Yes	No
153.	Is it always hard for you to make up your mind?	Yes	No
154.	Do you wish you always had someone at your side to advise you?	Yes	No
155.	Are you considered a clumsy person?	Yes	No
156.	Does it bother you to eat anywhere except in your own home?	Yes	No

Section N

157.	Do you feel alone and sad at a party?	Yes	No
158.	Do you usually feel unhappy and depressed?	Yes	No
159.	Do you often cry?	Yes	No
160.	Are you always miserable and blue?	Yes	No
161.	Does life look entirely hopeless?	Yes	No
162.	Do you often wish you were dead and away from it all?	Yes	No

Section O

163.	Does worrying continually get you down?	Yes	No
164.	Does worrying run in your family?	Yes	No
165.	Does every little thing get on your nerves and wear you out?	Yes	No

166.	Are you considered a nervous person?	Yes	No
167.	Does nervousness run in your family?	Yes	No
168.	Did you ever have a nervous breakdown?	Yes	No
169.	Did anyone in your family ever have a nervous breakdown?	Yes	No
170.	Were you ever a patient in a mental hospital (for your nerves?)	Yes	No
171.	Was anyone in your family ever a patient in a mental hospital (for their nerves)?	Yes	No

Section P

172.	Are you extremely shy or sensitive?	Yes	No
173.	Do you come from a shy or sensitive family?	Yes	No
174.	Are your feelings easily hurt?	Yes	No
175.	Does criticism always upset you?	Yes	No
176.	Are you considered a touchy person?	Yes	No
177.	Do people usually misunderstand you?	Yes	No

Section Q

178.	Do you have to be on your guard even with friends?	Yes	No
179.	Do you always do things on sudden impulse?	Yes	No
180.	Are you easily upset or irritated?	Yes	No
181.	Do you go to pieces if you don't constantly control yourself?	Yes	No

Interviewer's Comments

17. What was the respondent's race?

_____ White
_____ Black
_____ Brown
_____ Spoke Spanish only
_____ Other (specify)

18. Sex of respondent.

_____ Male
_____ Female

19.   Please write any comments about the interview here, including how it
went, what the surroundings were like, where the interview was
conducted, and any other observations you have.

**Unseen Community Project:
Life Course Interview
Downtown Hotel Residents**

1.   Were you raised by your parents in their home?
If no, who raised you?

Where?

2.   Were your parents divorced?

_____ Yes
_____ No
_____ Don't know
_____ Other (specify)

3.   What is the worst thing that happened when you were a child?
How old were you? _____
What effect did it have on your life?

4.   What is the best thing that happened when you were a child?
How old were you? _____
What effect did it have on your life?

5.   How old were you when your father died?

_____ (Age)
_____ Father not dead

6.   How old were you when your mother died?

                    _____ (Age)
                    _____ Mother not dead

7.   How old were you when you left home?

                    _____ (Age)
      Why did you leave home?

8.   How many times have you been married? _____

9.   What was your age at your *first* marriage? _____

10.   How long did the marriage last?

                    _____ Years
      If it was broken, why?

11.   What was your spouse's occupation?

12.   Did you have any children?

                    _____ Yes
                    _____ No
                    _____ Other (specify)
      If yes, how many? _____

13.   Was your marriage a happy one?

                    _____ Yes
                    _____ No
                    _____ Don't know
                    _____ Other (specify)
      Go to Question 24 if only one marriage)

14.   What was your age at your *second* marriage?

_____ Years

15.   How long did the marriage last?

_____ Years

If it was broken, why?

16.   What was your spouse's occupation?

17.   Did you have any children?

_____ Yes
_____ No
_____ Other (specify)

If yes, how many? _____

18.   Was your marriage a happy one?

_____ Yes
_____ No
_____ Don't know
_____ Other (specify)

Go to Question 24 if not a third marriage)

19.   What was your age at your *third* marriage?

_____ Years

20.   How long did the marriage last?

_____ Years

If it was broken, why?

21.   What was your spouse's occupation?

22. Did you have any children?

           _____ Yes
           _____ No
           _____ Other (specify)

If yes, how many? _____

23. Was your marriage a happy one?

           _____ Yes
           _____ No
           _____ Don't know
           _____ Other (specify)

24. Have you ever lived with a person of the opposite sex to whom you were not married?

           _____ Yes
           _____ No
           _____ Don't know
           _____ Other (specify)

Now I'd like to ask you some questions about your present living situation.

25. What do you enjoy most these days?

26. What are the chief problems in your life lately?

27. Are there any things about yourself or your living conditions that make life sort of difficult or unpleasant?

           _____ Yes
           _____ No
           _____ Don't know
           _____ Other (specify)

If yes, what are they?

28. Is there anything you could do a year ago that you can't do now that you miss doing?

         _____ Yes
         _____ No
         _____ Don't know
         _____ Other (specify)

If yes, what?

29. How about living alone? Do you have difficulties with it?

         _____ Yes
         _____ No
         _____ Don't know
         _____ Other (specify)

If yes, is that because you would like someone around for company or to help out with things?

30. Do you feel lonely very often?

         _____ Yes
         _____ No
         _____ Don't know
         _____ Other (specify)

If yes, at any particular time or just generally?

Since when?

What could make you less lonely?

31. Please give the first names of three friends:

(1) _____

    32. What about that friend do you like most?

    33. What quality of that person is the most important to your friendship?

34. (2) _____

    35. What about that friend do you like most?

    36. What quality of that person is the most important to your friendship?

37. (3) _____

    38. What about that friend do you like most?

    39. What quality of that person is the most important to your friendship?

40. During the past year or so, have you noticed any changes in the way your relatives, friends, or neighbors feel about you? Or the way they act toward you?

            _____ Yes
            _____ No
            _____ Don't know
            _____ Other (specify)

If yes, who is that?

What is the difference?

41. Have any of your relatives, friends or neighbors died recently?

            _____ Yes
            _____ No
            _____ Don't know
            _____ Other (specify)

If yes, who?   When?

Were you close to them?

Where did they live?

42. Do you use a bank?

            _____ Yes
            _____ No
            _____ Don't know
            _____ Other (specify)

If no, why not?

Now, I'd like to ask some questions about your health.

43. Have you gone to a doctor in the past year? (Regular doctor, chiropractor, foot specialist, etc.)

    _____ Yes
    _____ No
    _____ Don't know
    _____ Other (specify)

    If yes, what type?

44. Have you been a patient in a hospital in the past year?

    _____ Yes
    _____ No
    _____ Don't know
    _____ Other (specify)

    If yes, what type? (nursing home?)

45. Are you able to go out of doors?

    Can do without difficulty and without assistance. ____

    Can do with difficulty but still without the help of another person. ____

    Can do with difficulty and only with help of another person. ____

46. Are you able to walk up and down stairs?

    Can do without difficulty and without assistance. ____

    Can do with difficulty but still without the help of another person. ____

    Can do with difficulty and only with help of another person. ____

Bibliography

Abramson, J.H. "The Cornell Medical Index as an Epidemiological Tool." *American Journal of Public Health*, 56 (Feb., 1966):237-98.

Adams, F.M. "The Role of Old People in Santo Tomas Mazaltepec." In *Aging and Modernization*, edited by Donald O. Cowgill and Lowell D. Holmes. New York: Appleton-Century-Crofts, 1972.

Arth, M.J. "An Interdisciplinary View of the Aged in Ibo Culture." *Journal of Geriatric Psychiatry* 2:1 (1968):33-39.

Bahr, H.M. "The Gradual Disappearance of Skid Row," *Social Problems* 15:1 (1968):41-45.

Bateson, G. *Steps to an Ecology of Mind.* San Francisco: Chandler, 1972.

Benedict, R. *Patterns of Culture.* New York: Mentor, 1934.

Bennett, J.W. "Anticipation, Adaptation, and the Concept of Culture in Anthropology." *Science* 192 (1976):847-53.

Beresford, J.C. and A.M. Rivlin "The Multigenerational Family." Prepared for a Meeting on the Multigenerational Family at the University of Michigan Conference on Aging. Mimeographed. Ann Arbor, Michigan, 1969.

Berreman, G. "Ethnography: Method and Product." In *Introduction to Cultural Anthropology,* edited by James Clifton. Boston: Houghton Mifflin, 1968.

Bild, B. and R. Havighurst. "Senior Citizens in Great Cities: The Case of Chicago" *The Gerontologist* 16:1, Part II (1976).

Birren, J.E. "The Abuse of the Urban Aged." *Psychology Today* 3:10 (1970):37-38.

Blau, P.M. *Exchange and Power in Social Life.* New York: J. Wiley, 1964.

Blumberg, L., T.E. Shipley, Jr. and J.O. Moor. "The Skid Row Man and the Skid Row Status Community," *Quarterly Journal of Studies on Alcohol,* 32 (1971):909-41.

Bogue, D.J. *Skid-row in American Cities.* Chicago: University and Family Study Center, 1963.

Bohannan, P.J. "A Room of My Own." Unpublished manuscript.

Bohannan, P.J. and J.K. Eckert. *Food and Food-Related Health of Old People in Center City Hotels.* La Jolla, Ca.: Western Behavioral Sciences Institute, 1976.

Boissevain, J. "The Place of Non-groups in the Social Sciences." *Man (N.S.)* 3 (1968):542-56.

_____ . *Friend of Friends: Networks, Manipulators, and Coalitions.* Oxford: Basil Blackwell, 1974.

Bott, E. *Family and Social Networks.* London: Tavistock Publications, 1937.

Brice, D. "The Geriatric Ghetto." *San Francisco,* 12:9 (1970):70-72, 82.

Brodman, K., A.J. Erdmann, Jr., I. Lorge and H.G. Wolff. "The Cornell Medical Index-Health Questionnaire. II. As a Diagnostic Instrument," *Journal of the American Medical Association,* 145 (Jan. 20, 1951):152-57.

Brodman, K., A.J. Erdmann, Jr., I. Lorge, C.P. Gershenson and H.G. Wolff. "The Cornell Medical Index-Health Questionnaire. III. The Evaluation of Emotional Disturbances," *Journal of Clinical Psychology,* 8 (April, 1952):119-24.

Brodman, K., A.J. Erdmann, Jr., I. Lorge and H.W. Wolff. "The Cornell Medical Index-Health Questionnaire. VI. The Relation of Patients' Complaints to Age, Sex, Race, and Education," *Journal of Gerontology*, 8 (1953):339-42.

Butler, R.N. "Ageism: Another Form of Bigotry," *Gerontologist*, 9 (1969):243-46.

_____. *Why Survive? Being Old in America*. New York: Harper and Row, 1975.

Caplow, T., K.A. Lovald and S.E. Wallace. *A General Report on the Problem of Relocating the Population of the Lower Loop Redevelopment Area*. Multilith. Minneapolis: Minneapolis Housing and Redevelopment Authority, 1958.

Carp, F.M. "Housing and Living Environments of Older People." In *Handbook of Aging and the Social Sciences*, edited by R.H. Binstock and E. Shanas. New York: Van Nostrand Reinhold Company, 1976.

Cassel, J. and H.A. Tyroler. "Epidemiological Studies of Culture Change: I. Health Status and Recency of Industrialization," *Archives of Environmental Health*, 3 (1961):25-33.

Chance, N.A. "Conceptual and Methodological Problems in Cross-Cultural Health Research." *American Journal of Public Health* 52 (1962):410-17.

Clark, M. "Pattern of Aging Among the Elderly Poor of the Inner City," *The Gerontologist* Part II (Spring, 1971):58-66.

_____. "Cultural Values and Dependency in Later Life." In *Aging and Modernization*, edited by D.O. Cowgill and L.D. Holmes. New York: Appleton-Century-Crofts, 1972.

_____. "Contributions of Cultural Anthropology to the Study of the Aged." In *Cultural Illness and Health*, edited by Laura Nader and Thomas Maretzki. Anthropological Studies, No. 9. Washington: American Anthropological Association, 1973.

Clark, M. and B.G. Anderson, *Culture and Aging*. Springfield: Charles C. Thomas, 1967.

Clark, M. and M. Mendelson. "Mexican-American Aged in San Francisco: A Case Description," *Gerontologist* 9:2, Pt. 1 (1969):90-95.

Cohen, A.K. and H. Hodges. "Characteristics of the Lower Blue-Collar-Class." *Social Problems* 10(4) (1963):303-334.

Cohen, R. "Generalization in Ethnology." In *A Handbook of Method in Cultural Anthropology*, edited by Raoul Naroll and Ronald Cohen. Garden City: Natural History Press, 1970.

Collins, C.J.L. *Social Service Needs of the Aged. Social and Rehabilitation Service*. Washington, D.C.: U.S. Department of Health, 1972.

Cowgill, D.O. and L.D. Holmes, ed. *Aging and Modernization*. New York: Appleton-Century-Crofts, 1972.

Croog, S.H. "Educational Level and Responses to a Health Questionnaire." *Human Organization* 20 (1961):65-69.

Cumming, E. and W. Henry. *Growing Old: The Process of Disengagement*. New York: Basic Books, 1961.

D'Arcy, A.M. "Elderly Hotel Residents and Their Social Networks in Downtown San Diego." Masters thesis, San Diego State University, 1976.

Denzin, N.K. *The Research Act*. Chicago: Aldine, 1970.

Dewey, J. and A.F. Bentley. *Knowing and the Known.* Boston: Beacon Press, 1960.

Dowd, J.J. "Aging and Exchange: A Preface to Theory." *Journal of Gerontology* 30(1975):584-94.

Dubos, R. *Man Adapting.* New Haven: Yale University Press, 1963.

Durkheim, E. *The Division of Labor in Society.* New York: Free Press, 1947.

Ehrlich, P. *St. Louis' "Invisible" Elderly: Needs and Characteristics of Aged "Single Room Occupancy" Downtown Hotel Residents.* St. Louis: Institute of Applied Gerontology, St. Louis University, 1976.

Emmerson, R.M. "Power-dependence Relations." *American Sociological Review* 27(1962):31-41.

Epstein, A.L. "Gossips, Norms, and Social Networks." In *Social Networks in Urban Situations,* edited by J. Clyde Mitchell. Manchester: Manchester University Press, 1969.

Erdmann, A.J., K. Brodman, I. Lorge and H.G. Wolff. "The Cornell Medical Index-Health Questionnaire. V. The Outpatient Admitting Department of a General Hospital." *Journal of the American Medical Association* 149(June 7, 1952):550-51.

Erickson, R.J. *Social Profiles of San Diego: I. A Social Area Analysis.* La Jolla, Ca.: Western Behavioral Sciences Institute, 1973.

Erickson, R.J. and J.K. Eckert. "The Elderly Poor in Downtown San Diego Hotels," *Gerontologist* 17:5(1977):440-446.

Fried, M. "Land Tenure, Geography and Ecology in the Contact of Cultures." *American Journal of Economics and Sociology* 11:1(1952).

_____. *The Evolution of Political Society*. New York: Random House, 1967.

Friedmann, E.A. "The Impact of Aging on the Social Structure." In *The Handbook of Social Gerontology*, edited by C. Tibbitts. Chicago: University of Chicago Press, 1960.

Gans, H. *The Urban Villagers*. New York: Free Press, 1962.

Geertz, C. *The Interpretation of Culture*. New York: Basic Books, 1973.

Glaser, B.G. and A.L. Strauss. *The Discovery of Grounded Theory*. Chicago: Aldine Publishing Co., 1967.

Gorer, G. *The American People: A Study in National Character*. New York: W.W. Norton and Company, 1945.

Grinker, R. *Toward a Unified Theory of Human Behavior*. New York: Basic Books, 1965.

Gutmann, D. "The Hunger of Old Men." *Trans-Action* 9(1971):55-66.

Haberman, P. "The Reliability and Validity of the Data." In *Poverty and Health*, edited by J. Kosa, et al. Cambridge: Harvard University Press, 1969.

Hall, E.T. *Beyond Culture*. Garden City, N.Y.: Anchor Press/Doubleday, 1976.

Hamer, J.H. "Aging in a Gerontocratic Society: The Sidamo of Southwest Ethiopia." In *Aging and Modernization*, edited by D.O. Cowgill and L.D. Holmes. New York: Appleton-Century-Crofts, 1972.

Hannerz, U. *Soulside: Inquiries into Ghetto Culture and Community*. New York: Columbia University Press, 1969.

Harris, M. *The Rise of Anthropological Theory.* New York: Thomas Y. Crowell Co., 1968.

Hauser, P.M. "Aging and World-wide Population Change." In *Handbook of Aging and the Social Sciences,* edited by R.H. Binstock and E. Shanas. New York: Van Nostrand Reinhold Company, 1976.

Havighurst, R. "A Social Psychological Perspective on Aging." *The Gerontologist* VIII (1968).

Hayner, N.S. *Hotel Life.* Asheville, North Carolina: University of North Carolina Press, 1936.

Herbolsheimer, H. and B.L. Ballard. "Multiple Screening in Evaluation of Entering College and University Students." *Journal of the American Medical Association* 166(Feb. 1, 1958):444-53.

Hoke, B. "Promotive Medicine and the Phenomenon of Health." *Archives of Environmental Health* 16(1968):269-78.

————. "Health and Healthing." *Ekistics* 220 (March, 1974).

Holmes, L.D. "The Role and Status of the Aged in a Changing Samoa." In *Aging and Modernization,* edited by D.O. Cowgill and L.D. Holmes. New York: Appleton-Century-Crofts, 1972.

Homans, G. *The Human Group.* New York: Harcourt Brace, 1950.

Honigmann, J.J. "The Personal Approach in Cultural Anthropology Research." *Current Anthropology* 17:2(1970):243-61.

Hsu, F.L.K., ed. "American Core Value and National Character." In *Psychological Anthropology.* New Edition. Cambridge, Mass.: Schenkman Publishing Co., 1959.

_____ . *Psychological Anthropology: Approaches to Culture and Personality.* Homewood, Illinois: Dorsey Press, 1961.

Insel, P.M. and R.H. Moos, ed. "The Social Environment." In *Health and the Social Environment.* Lexington, Mass.: D.C. Heath and Co. 1974.

Jacobs, J. *The Death and Life of Great American Cities.* New York: Vintage Books, 1961.

Jorgens, R. "An Intimate Glimpse into the Life of the SRO Elderly." Paper presented at the Second Annual Conference on SRO Elderly. St. Louis: St. Louis University Institute of Applied Gerontology, May, 1976.

Kalish, R.A. "Of Children and Grandfathers: A Speculative Essay on Dependency." *The Gerontologist* 7:1(1967):65-69, 79.

Kark, E., A. Zaslany and B. Ward. "The Health of the Undergraduate Student on Entry to the Hebrew University in Jerusalem." *Israel Medical Journal.* 22(1963):147-155.

Kelly, J.G. "Ecological Constraints on Mental Health Services." *American Psychologist.* 21(1966):535-39.

Kleemeier, R.W., ed. *Aging and Leisure.* New York: Oxford University Press, 1961.

Kluckhohn, C. *Mirror for Man.* New York: Whittlesey House, 1949.

_____ . "Culture and Behavior." In *Handbook of Social Psychology,* edited by G. Lindzey. New York: Addison-Wesley, 1954.

Laufer, L.G. "Cultural Problems Encountered in Use of the Cornell Index Among Okinawan Natives." *American Journal of Psychiatry* 109(1953):861-864.

Lawton, M.P. "The Screening Value of the Cornell Medical Index." *Journal of Consulting Psychology* 23(1959):352-56.

_____ . "Social Ecology and the Health of Older People." *American Journal of Public Health* 64:3(1974):257-60.

Lawton, M.P. and M.H. Kleban. "The Aged Resident of the Inner City." *The Gerontologist* 11(1971).

LeVine, R.A. "Intergenerational Tensions and Extended Family Structures in Africa." In *Social Structure and the Family: Generational Relations,* edited by E. Shanas and G. Streib. Englewood Cliffs: Prentice-Hall, 1965.

Lewin, K. *Field Theory in Social Science.* New York: Harper and Row, 1951.

Liebow, E. *Tally's Corner.* Boston: Little, Brown, 1967.

Linton, R. *The Cultural Background of Personality.* New York: Century, 1945.

Lofland, L.H. *A World of Strangers.* New York: Basic Books, 1973.

Lopata, H.Z. "Support Systems of Elderly Urbanites: Chicago of the 1970s." *The Gerontologist* 15:1, Part 1(1975):35-41.

Lowenthal, M.F. "Social Isolation and Mental Illness in Old Age." *American Sociological Review* 29(1964):54-70.

Lowenthal, M.F. and P.L. Berkmann and Associates. *Aging and Mental Disorders in San Francisco.* San Francisco: Jossey-Bass, 1967.

Lowenthal, M.F. and B. Robinson. "Social Networks and Isolation." In *Handbook of Aging and the Social Sciences,* edited by R.H. Binstock and E. Shanas. New York: Van Nostrand Reinhold Company, 1976.

Maas, H.S. and J.A. Kuypers. *From Thirty to Seventy.* San Francisco: Jossey-Bass, 1974.

Maddox, G.L. "Self-Assessment of Health Status: A Longitudinal Study of Elderly Subjects." *Journal of Chronic Diseases* 176(1964):449-460.

Maddox, G.L. and E.B. Douglas. "Self Assessment of Health: A Longitudinal Study of Elderly Subjects." *Journal of Health and Social Behavior* 14(1973):18-93.

Martin, J. and Doran, A. "Perception of Retirement: Time and Season" Pilkington Research Project on Retirement, Liverpool, England, 1967.

Matarazzo, R.G., J.D. Matarazzo and G. Saslow. "The Relationships Between Medical and Psychiatric Systems." *Journal of Abnormal and Social Psychology* 62(1961):55-61.

Mead, M. *And Keep Your Powder Dry.* New York: William Morrow and Company, 1943.

Mechanic, D. *Medical Sociology.* New York: The Free Press, 1968.

Miller, S.M. and F. Riessman. "The Working Class Subculture: A New View." *Social Problems* 9:1(1961):86-97.

Mitchell, J.C. *Social Networks in Urban Situations.* Manchester: University of Manchester Press, 1966.

Monroe, R.T., F.E. Whiskin, P. Bonacich and W.O. Jewell, III. "The Cornell Medical Index Questionnaire as a Measure of Health in Older People." *Journal of Gerontology* 20 (1965):18-22.

Mulanaphy, J.M. "1972-73 Survey of Retired TIAA-CREF Annuitants." *Statistical Report, Teachers Insurance and Annuity Association, College Retirement Equities Fund.* New York, 1974.

Munsell, M.R. "Functions of the Aged Among the Salt River Pima." In *Aging and Modernization,* edited by D.O. Cowgill and L.D. Holmes. New York: Appleton-Century-Crofts, 1972.

Murray, H.A. *Exploration in Personality.* New York: Oxford University Press, 1938.

Nadel, S.F. "Witchcraft in Four African Societies: An Essay on Comparison." *American Anthropologist* 54 (1952):18-29.

Neugarten, B.L. and Associates, ed. *Personality in Middle and Late Life.* New York: Atherton, 1964.

Niebanck, P.L. and J. Pope. *The Elderly in Older Urban Areas: Problems of Adaptation and the Effects of Relocation.* Philadelphia: Institute for Environmental Studies, University of Pennsylvania, 1965.

Parsons, T. *The Social System.* New York: Free Press of Glencoe, 1951.

Pelto, P.J. and G. Pelto. "Ethnography: The Fieldwork Enterprise." In *Handbook of Social and Cultural Anthropology,* edited by J.J. Honigmann. Chicago: Rand McNally, 1973.

Pervin, L.A. "Performance and Satisfaction as a Function of Individual-Environment Fit." In *Issues in Social Ecology,* edited by R.H. Moos and P.M. Insel. Palo Alto: National Press Books, 1974.

Plath, D.W. "Japan: The After Years." In *Aging and Modernization,* edited by D.O. Cowgill and L.D. Holmes. New York: Appleton-Century-Crofts, 1972.

Pollak, O. *Social Adjustment in Old Age: A Research Planning Report.* Bulletin 59. New York: Social Science Research Council, 1948.

Redfield, R. *The Little Community.* Chicago: University of Chicago Press, 1953.

Reiss, A.J., Jr. *The Police and the Public.* New Haven: Yale University Press, 1971.

Riesman, D. "The Suburban Dislocation." *The Annals* 34(1957):123-46.

Riley, M.W. and A. Foner. *Aging and Society.* Vol. 1. *An Inventory of Research Findings.* New York: Russell Sage Foundation, 1968.

Ross, J.K. *Old People, New Lives: Community Creation in a Retirement Residence.* Chicago: University of Chicago Press, 1977.

Rose, A.M. "Interest in the Living Arrangement of the Urban Unattached." *American Journal of Sociology* 53 (May, 1948).

Rosenberg, G.S. *The Worker Grows Old: Poverty and Isolation in the City.* San Francisco: Jossey-Bass, 1970.

Rosow, I. *Social Integration of the Aged.* New York: Free Press, 1967.

Ryan, S. "Chambermaids: A Profile of Some Women's Work." *Social Policy* March/April, 1977:36-40.

Ryser, C. and Shelton, A. "Retirement and Health." *Journal of American Geriatric Society* 17 (1969):180-190.

Saldo, B.J. and G.G. Myer. "The Changing Profile of Living Arrangements Among the Elderly, 1960-1970." *The Gerontologist* 15:5, Part II (1975).

Sargent, F. "Man-Environment Problems for Public Health." *American Journal of Public Health* 62:5(1972):628-33.

Scotch, N.A. and H.J. Geiger. "An Index of Symptoms and Disease in Zulu Culture." *Human Organization* 22(1963-64):304-11.

Service, E. "Indian-European Relations in Colonial Latin America." *American Anthropologist* 57(1953):411-25.

_____ . *Primitive Social Organization.* New York: Random House, 1962.

Shanas, E. *The Health of Older People: A Social Survey.* Cambridge: Harvard University Press, 1962.

Shanas, E., P. Townsend, D. Wedderburn, H. Friis, P. Milhoj and J. Stehouwer, ed. *Old People in Three Industrial Societies.* New York: Atherton, 1968.

Shapiro, J.H. "Single-Room Occupancy: Community of the Alone." *Social Work* 11(October, 1966).

_____ . "Dominant Leaders Among Slum Hotel Residents." *American Journal of Orthopsychiatry* 39(July, 1969).

_____ . "Reciprocal Dependence Between Single-Room Occupancy Managers and Tenants." *Social Work.* 15 (July, 1970).

_____ . *Communities of the Alone.* New York: Association Press, 1971.

Shaw, C. *The Jack Roller: A Delinquent Boy's Own Story.* Chicago: University of Chicago Press, 1930.

Sheppard, H.L. "Work and Retirement." In *Handbook of Aging and the Social Sciences,* edited by R.H. Binstock and E. Shanas. New York: Van Nostrand Reinhold Company, 1976.

_____. "Age and Migration Factors in Socioeconomic Conditions of Urban Black and White Women." In *New Perspectives on Older Workers,* edited by H.L. Sheppard. Kalamazoo: Upjohn Institute for Employment Research, 1971.

Siegal, H. *Outposts of the Forgotten; Lifeways of Socially Terminal People in Slum Hotels and Single Room Occupancy Tenements.* New Jersey: Transaction Books, 1978.

Simmel, G. *The Sociology of George Simmel.* Edited by K.H. Wolff. New York: Macmillan, 1950. (English translation of G. Simmel, *Die Grossstadte und das Geistesleben Die Grossstadte,* 1903.)

Simmons, L.W. *The Role of the Aged in Primitive Societies.* New Haven: Yale University Press, 1945.

Simon, H.A. *Models of Man: Explorations in the Western Educational Tradition.* New York: Wiley, 1957.

Spencer, P. *The Samburu: A Study of Gerontology in a Nomadic Tribe.* Berkeley and Los Angeles: University of California Press, 1965.

Spiegel, J.P. "A Model for Relationships Among Systems." In *Toward a Unified Theory of Human Behavior,* edited by R. Grinker. New York: Basic Books, 1956.

Spradley, J. *You Owe Yourself a Drunk.* Boston: Little, Brown, 1970.

Steinhardt, R.W., F.D. Zeman, J. Tuchman and I. Lorge. "Appraisal of Physical and Mental Health of the Elderly; Use of Cornell Medical Index and Supplementary Health Questionnaire." *Journal of the American Medical Association* 151 (January 31, 1953):378-82.

Stephens, B.J. *Loners, Losers, and Lovers: Elderly Tenants in a Slum Hotel.* Seattle: University of Washington Press, 1976.

Steward, J. *Theory of Culture Change.* Urbana: University of Illinois Press, 1955.

Stokols, D. "Environmental Psychology." *Annual Review of Psychology* 29(1978):253-95.

Suttles, G.D. "Urban Ethnography: Situational and Normative Accounts." In *Annual Review of Sociology,* edited by A. Inkeles, J. Coleman and N. Smelser. Vol. 2. Palo Alto: Annual Review, Inc., 1976.

Thompson, W.E. and G.F. Streib. "Situational Determinants: Health and Economic Deprivation in Retirement." *Journal of Social Issues.* 14:2(1958):18-34.

Tissue, T. "Old Age, Poverty and the Central City." *Aging and Human Development.* 2(1971):235-48.

Tonnies, F. *Community and Society (Gemeinschaft und Gesellschaft).* Translated by C.P. Loomis. New York: Harper and Row, 1963.

Tibbitts, C. and J.L. Schmelzer. "New Directions in Aging and Their Research Implications." *Welfare in Review* 3:2(1965):8-14.

Townsend, P. "Measuring Incapacity for Self-Care." In *Processes of Aging, II,* edited by R.H. Williams, C. Tibbitts and W. Donahue. New York: Atherton Press, 1963.

U.S. Department of Commerce, Bureau of the Census. *Demographic Aspects of Aging and the Old Population in the United States.* Current Population Reports, Special Studies, Series P-23, No. 59, May, 1976.

Vayda, A. "Maori Conquests in Relation to the New Zealand Environment." *Journal of Polynesian Society.* 65 (1956):204-11.

_____. "A Re-examination of Northwest Coast Economic Systems." *Transactions of the New York Academy of Sciences* Ser. 2, 23:7(1961):618-24.

von Mering, O. "An Anthromedical Profile of Aging — Retirement from Life into Active Ill Health." *Journal of Geriatric Psychiatry* 3:1(1969):61-81.

Wallace, A.F.C. "Mental Illness, Biology, and Culture." In *Psychological Anthropology*, edited by F.L.K. Hsu. New edition. Cambridge, Mass.: Schenkman Publishing Co., 1972.

Wallace, S.E. *Skid Row as a Way of Life.* Totowa, N.J.: Bedminister Press, 1965.

Walsh, B. *Theories of Person-Environment Interaction: Implications for the College Students.* Monograph 10. The American College Testing Program, 1973.

Whyte, W.F. *Street Corner Society: The Social Structure of an Italian Slum.* Chicago: University of Chicago Press, 1943.

Williams, R.H. *American Society: Sociological Interpretations.* 3rd edition. New York: Alfred A. Knopf, Inc., 1970.

Williams, R.H. and C.G. Wirths. *Lives Through the Years.* New York: Atherton Press, 1965.

Wirth, L. "Urbanism as a Way of Life." *American Journal of Sociology* 44:1(1938):1-24.

Wolf, E. "Closed Corporate Peasant Communities in Mesoamerica and Central Java." *Southwestern Journal of Anthropology* (1957):1-18.

_____ . *Peasants*. Englewood Cliffs, N.J.: Prentice Hall, 1966.

Woodruff, D. and J. Birren. *Aging: Scientific Perspectives and Social Issues*. New York: Van Nostrand Co., 1975.

Zorbaugh, H.W. *The Golden Coast and the Slums*. Chicago: University of Chicago Press, 1926.

This book was set in Edinburgh type on
the Singer Photomix Phototypesetter
7450 by Pam Muncey, Word Processing,
San Diego State University. Text paper is
55lb Glatfelter Natural.